THE
BATTLE
OF THE
BULGE

D0872435

THE
BATTLE
OF THE
BULGE
HITLER'S FINAL GAMBLE
IN WESTERN EUROPE

MARTIN KING

Acknowledgements

For all Battle of the Bulge veterans past and present.

This book is dedicated to my wife Freya, kids Allycia and Ashley, all family members and Battle of the Bulge veteran, dearly respected friend John Schaffner, Scout, Battery B, 589th Field Artillery Battalion, 106th Infantry Division. Many thanks to John Turing and Arcturus Publishing for asking me to write this volume. Also thanks to former General Graham Hollands, former Naval Commander Jeff Barta and former 101st Airborne Commander Robert Campbell. Thanks also to Mike Collins for his support and assistance.

This edition published in 2019 by Arcturus Publishing Limited
26/27 Bickels Yard, 151–153 Bermondsey Street,
London SE1 3HA

Copyright © Arcturus Holdings Limited

All rights reserved. No part of this publication may be reproduced, stored in a retrieval system, or transmitted, in any form or by any means, electronic, mechanical, photocopying, recording or otherwise, without prior written permission in accordance with the provisions of the Copyright Act 1956 (as amended). Any person or persons who do any unauthorised act in relation to this publication may be liable to criminal prosecution and civil claims for damages.

AD006662UK

Printed in the UK

Contents

Foreword

WITH EACH GENERATION, EPIC HISTORICAL events seem to recede into the background and slowly fade from memory. But some moments in history are just too pivotal and important ever to be forgotten. This story, about the Battle of the Bulge, is one such event.

In the winter of 1944–5 I was stationed in the Ardennes, one of thousands of American soldiers desperately trying to understand what was going on around us and, most importantly of all, fighting to survive. Although we didn't know it at the time, my unit, the 106th Infantry Division, stood directly in the path of the main German assault. I now realize that the German attack, which comprised three Panzer armies and their supporting troops, should almost certainly have succeeded. This even surprised the American commanders, from General Eisenhower down to the platoon leaders on the front line. The few who saw it coming had been disbelieved and ignored.

How could this have happened?

The German attack focused on three American divisions, which presented a very weak defensive line. Two of them, the 99th and 106th Infantry divisions, had no combat experience, and the third, the 28th Infantry Division, had recently incurred significant losses in the Battle of the Hürtgen Forest. These divisions were assigned to defend a line at least three times the length of any they had been trained for. It was a recipe for disaster.

At the outset of battle on 16 December 1944, the American units took an awful beating while attempting to overcome impossible odds. It's now clear that they had become engaged in one of the largest land battles fought on the Western Front, for which the Allied side was poorly prepared and badly set up. After all these years you might think that interest would be on the wane, but more and more people want to discover the truth about the events of World War II. Historians have written thousands of words on the subject, and keep coming up with fresh explanations about what happened and why.

The aim of this book is to give the reader an understanding of the Battle of the Bulge and to explain the part it played in shaping the subsequent history of World War II and beyond. There's an old saying among soldiers who have experienced combat: 'When the first shot is fired, you throw the book away.' Perhaps that's an exaggeration, but when you're on the front line you don't have time to consult a book to work out your next move. No book can prepare you for the reality of combat. However, in this one, Martin King provides a pretty good idea of what it was like to be there.

John Schaffner
Scout, 106th Infantry Division, US Army

Preface

I MOVED TO BELGIUM FROM the United Kingdom in 1982. My fascination with the Battle of the Bulge began when I met my first World War II veteran back in 1988. He was a Boston man, quiet, unassuming and very articulate, even if he did have a peculiar inflection in his speech. When he spoke it was in measured, precise sentences that disguised any emotion he may or may not have felt as he revisited his old battleground. 'What do you know about the battle, Martin?' he asked. 'Bits and bats,' I replied, my attention distracted, attempting to avoid erratic Belgian drivers and imminent death. 'Look at this,' he said as he lifted his leg, removed his Hush Puppy and revealed what appeared to be at least four pairs of socks. I glanced to my right but didn't notice anything unusual, except it was July and I remember thinking four pairs of socks was a bit excessive for the time of year. My focus remained on the road because I hadn't been driving all that long. 'Can you see that?' he asked, pointing at his foot. I looked again and swerved to avoid an approaching truck. Finally, I pulled over into a small layby, put the car in neutral and breathed a huge sigh of relief. Then I looked down. 'What the f... sorry, but your foot... it doesn't have... does it hurt?' He didn't have any toes, just small stumps where they had once been. 'Naah, lost 'em all down here somewhere, maybe we can find 'em and stick 'em back on, eh buddy.' Beneath a variegated thatch of white, brown and grey hair, a wry smile appeared to crack his grained visage that erupted into a full-blown cackle. I could tell that I was going to get on well with this guy and I was right.

Then his brow furrowed as he went on to say, 'We get bad winters over in Boston you know, really bad sometimes.' I didn't know, but hailing from the frozen north of the United Kingdom I knew what a bad winter was. He continued, 'I've never been afraid of cold weather, son. After the war I got married and in 1953 we moved to Florida. I thought it was a good idea to get some warm weather after this thing. Been there ever since. Sunshine, and beautiful weather almost every day. But you know what?' He shook his head ever so slightly and his eyes welled. 'Tried everything son, but I still can't get my goddam toes warm.' 'But you don't have...' I thought better of it and decided to simply listen and absorb, and I've been doing that ever since.

The Bostonian is what sparked my interest. Since then I have met and interviewed innumerable World War II veterans, and read many well-written books on the subject by many notable historians in multiple languages. I've even written a few myself.

Martin King,
2019

Introduction

THE BATTLE OF THE BULGE was the largest land battle in American military history and one of the most decisive and significant engagements of World War II. Seventy-five years after the battle, it's important to remember that all participants endured some of the harshest climactic conditions ever experienced in the western theatre. Temperatures frequently dipped below -28°C, and many inadequately prepared Americans ultimately succumbed to disabling weather-related maladies such as hypothermia, trenchfoot and frostbite. But it's also important to remember that pure dogged resilience and tenacity, combined with the impromptu acumen of certain individuals, resulted in a resounding victory for the Allies and a crushing defeat for the Third Reich. Their sacrifices should never be disregarded. As long as historians continue to write about the subject, these soldiers will not be forgotten and their experiences will inspire future generations.

Who can write anything new about the Battle of the Bulge? Most military historians and armchair generals acknowledge that the Battle of the Bulge was a bitter struggle of attrition and decimation, characterized by terrible weather and inhumanely freezing conditions. Both sides incurred high losses in the winter of 1944–45, with the American forces sustaining more casualties during this encounter than in any previously during the war. Numbers may vary but contemporary estimates agree that US forces suffered around 10,276 KIA (killed in action), 47,493 wounded and 23,218 MIA (missing in action). The German army incurred 12,652 KIA, 38,600 wounded and 30,000 MIA. British casualties were approximately 200 KIA, 969 wounded and 239 MIA. The battle cost the lives of around 3,000 civilians.

One volume isn't enough to cover everything that occurred during this huge battle, but with respect to the chronological timeline of events, I will hopefully provide some new perspectives from the ground up through the voices of witnesses, to give the reader a feel for what it was really like to be there. The Battle of the Bulge, sometimes called the Ardennes Offensive, began on 16 December 1944 and ended one month later on 16 January 1945. It was Germany's last major offensive action of World War II, launched as a desperate attempt to push back, or at least halt, the Allied advance eastwards after D-Day.

Over the past 30 years I've written seven books about World War II and interviewed innumerable veterans from all sides. I've visited the sites I write about, too. Not all historians do this, but knowing the lay of the land is imperative as far as I'm concerned and it's fair to say that I know the Ardennes intimately. That does not make me an expert. Military enthusiasts are precisely that, enthusiastic. However, authors don't always get everything right. I don't think there is such a thing as a true 'expert' in military history because all points are subjective and debatable, and that is what makes it fascinating.

The perspectives of men and women who were there at the time dominate all my books, and not many have anything good to say about combat and killing. At least they tell it from the ground up. My remit is, and has always been, to preserve as many of these personal experiences as is humanly possible, and I'm not the only one who does this, just one of the many who cares about history.

The Battle of the Bulge is in my opinion a very human story, a story of tragedy and ultimately victory best related by soldiers and civilians who witnessed it first-hand. Within these pages are the last of the best and the best of the last. We shall never see their like again.

I live roughly one hour north of the place where the infamous Battle of the Bulge occurred in the bitter winter of 1944–45. I digress, although I'm not a particularly fervent fan of Belgium as a whole, I love the Ardennes. It's a sedate and very tranquil place these days. A place of stunning pastoral scenery, where lush green forests, hills and deep valleys are bisected by beautifully picturesque rivers and streams meandering through age-old towns, villages and hamlets. It's a veritable haven of peace and relaxation. But it wasn't always like this. If bricks and mortar could talk they would have a remarkable story to tell. It's a shame that these days most people think that the 'Battle of the Bulge' is a weight-loss programme. However, few authors can claim to really know the Ardennes region as well as I do.

A popular misconception regarding the Ardennes is that it is one 'big pine forest' and the Germans were hiding in between the trees. This was most definitely not the case.

The terrain in each of the three main sectors where the battle occurred varies considerably. In the northern sector one can find deep valleys, rivers and precipitous hills, and just north of the Amblève valley there are gentle rolling pastures and plateaus that are referred to as the 'high fens'. There are a few sizeable cities in this region. One of the most important during the great battle was the German-speaking city of Sankt Vith that still had rail links to Germany in 1944 and was arguably more important than Bastogne.

In the heart of the Ardennes is the city of Bastogne. It rests on a high plateau where seven roads converge. There are a few planted woodlands close by and a lot of arable farmland. The southern sector incorporates the Duchy of Luxembourg, but I should point out that the province of Luxembourg where Bastogne is situated is irrefutably Belgian territory. Apparently, the population of Luxembourg consume more beef per capita than any other people in the world. This fact has absolutely nothing to do with the content of this volume but I couldn't help myself. Both Belgium and Luxembourg are bordered to the east by Germany. At least two locations along the Ardennes front were referred to by US troops who fought there as 'Skyline Drive'. Author John McManus wrote an excellent book titled *Alamo in the Ardennes* but there are few locations in the region that could have qualified for that title.

The Kingdom of Belgium has a population of around 11 million and three official languages. Dutch in the north, French in the southern and Ardennes region, and German in the eastern provinces. There are many indigenous dialects of both French and Dutch that have the capacity to confuse and confound all but the locals who speak them. The Duchy of Luxembourg also has three official languages: Luxembourgish, French and German. Some Germans claim that Luxembourgish (*Letzeburgisch*) is the epicentre of the original Germanic language that was allegedly spoken by Charlemagne and his Franks. That's probably one reason why the Third Reich was quick to annex Luxembourg in 1942.

At the time of writing I have spent over 30 years examining this intractable terrain, meticulously inspecting the remains of foxholes, bomb craters, bullet holes in masonry and other evidence of the massive battle that occurred there all those years ago. Having spent time in the company of noble World War II veterans who knew a very different Ardennes to the one I know today, I think it's time to give them a voice in these pages. It's fair to say that I do know this subject quite well.

Evidence is vital to a battlefield historian, and thankfully there's still plenty of it to be found in the Ardennes. Apart from having read virtually everything that's ever been written about the battle in English, I have also read French, Dutch and German versions. Combining and cross-referencing this information with information collected from the many veterans, archives and private collections, I think it's high time that I wrote my take on the battle.

In my previous publications I've written about various American divisions and certain individuals, and now I'm going to combine that information into one comprehensive volume. It will relay the story and hopefully help the reader to experience the battle through the eyes of the noble veterans, most of whom I interviewed personally. I hope that you enjoy it and keep me supplied with good quality single malt whisky (one glass a night strictly for medicinal purposes, whether I need it or not).

Martin King, Emmy Award Winning Author

Previous books:
Voices of the Bulge
The Tigers of Bastogne
To war with the 4th
The fighting 30th – they called them Roosevelt's SS
Warriors of the 106th
Searching for Augusta
Lost Voices

CHAPTER ONE

We're on a roll

YOUNG JIM COOLEY WROTE A valedictory note to his mother in Oklahoma when his division left the United States to sail into the grey, spuming North Atlantic to run the gauntlet of inclement weather, German U-boats and numerous other obstacles that could potentially impede their progress. That was October 1944 and he was with the 106th Infantry Division, who had received an invitation from Uncle Sam to participate in World War II. 'You're going to be mighty proud of your son, Ma,' wrote Jim. 'I'm going to be the first GI to cross the Rhine River.' He would indeed be one of the first, but it wouldn't be exactly as he had envisaged.

In the summer of 1944 after the breakout from Normandy the Allies had charged rapaciously across France and Belgium, facing largely ineffectual opposition. The pervading mood at SHAEF (Supreme Headquarters Allied Expeditionary Force) was joyous, even celebratory, but to some extent the recent successes had created a false sense of security. Now more than ever the Allies needed clear directives from cohesive and reliable command. The core problem was that the higher echelons

SITUATION WITH GERMAN PLAN OF ATTACK

15 December 1944

XXXX
FIRST
CRERAR (CAN.)

Antwerp

6th PANZER AR[
OBJECTIVE AR]

XXXXX
21
MONTGOMERY (UK)

SECOND
XXXX
NINTH

5th PANZER ARMY
OBJECTIVE AREA

XXXX
NINTH
SIMPSON(US)

21
XXXXX
12

Namur

NINT
XXX
FIR

BELGI[

FRANCE

0	10	20	30	40

Miles

Kilometres

0	10	20	30	40

XXXXXX
SHAEF
EISENHOWER (US)
(FWD. IN REIMS)

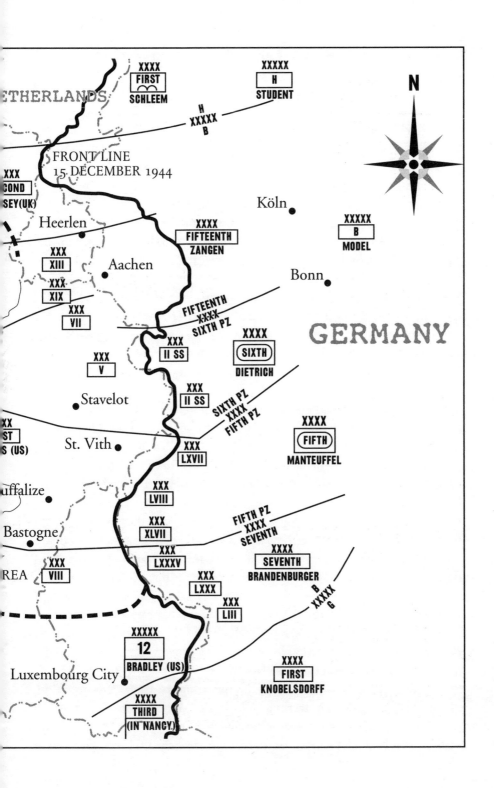

N

NETHERLANDS

XXXX
FIRST
SCHLEEM

XXXXX
H
STUDENT

H
XXXXX
B

FRONT LINE
15 DECEMBER 1944

XXX
COND
SEY(UK)

Köln

XXXXX
B
MODEL

Heerlen

XXX
XIII

Aachen

XXXX
FIFTEENTH
ZANGEN

Bonn

XXX
XIX

XXX
VII

FIFTEENTH
XXXX
SIXTH PZ

GERMANY

XXX
II SS

XXXX
SIXTH
DIETRICH

XXX
V

Stavelot

XXX
II SS

SIXTH PZ
XXXX
FIFTH PZ

XX
ST
S (US)

St. Vith

XXX
LXVII

XXXX
FIFTH
MANTEUFFEL

uffalize

XXX
LVIII

Bastogne

XXX
XLVII

FIFTH PZ
XXXX
SEVENTH

XXX
LXXXV

XXXX
SEVENTH
BRANDENBURGER

REA

XXX
VIII

XXX
LXXX

B
XXXXX
G

XXX
LIII

XXXXX
12
BRADLEY (US)

Luxembourg City

XXXX
FIRST
KNOBELSDORFF

XXXX
THIRD
(IN NANCY)

couldn't agree on a feasible way forward and opinions were often swayed by the pervasive triumphalist euphoria.

For example, *Time* magazine's war correspondent Charles Christian Wertenbaker recorded his observations and captured the moment when Paris was liberated in August 1944. 'I have seen the faces of young people in love and the faces of old people at peace with their God. I have never seen in any face such joy as radiated from the faces of the people of Paris this morning. This is no day for restraint, and I could not write with restraint if I wanted to.'

Darel Parker, Company C, 1st Battalion, 12th Infantry Regiment, 4th Infantry Division, joined his unit at Camp Gordon Johnston in Florida. He said, 'We moved from there to South Carolina, then to New Jersey and then to England. From England, we went to France, and then to Normandy on D-Day. The water was rough, but we made it and went on to cross the flooded areas. Some of the water there was six or seven feet deep, and with all the equipment we were carrying, it wasn't very easy. We then attacked on to Cherbourg and through the hedgerows. Then we went to Bloody Mortain, St Lô, and on to Paris, which was a story in itself.'

A member of General Eisenhower's intelligence staff had audaciously stated for the record that, 'Victory in Europe is within sight, almost within reach.' The 1st Army chief of intelligence went one step further, declaring 'We're on a roll here,' and predicted that it was unlikely that organized German resistance would continue beyond 1 December 1944. It all sounded too good to be true, and of course it was. But first the Allied commanders had to collectively agree on how they were going to continue taking the fight to the Nazis. The Allied commanders made too many assumptions at the time, because the enemy may have been decisively defeated in Normandy but they were not a spent force.

Fifty-five-year-old Eisenhower had already achieved a gargantuan feat by managing to weld the armies of different nations together into a formidable fighting force, the like of which Europe had never seen before. He had displayed a remarkable skill for diplomacy and patience in the face of often punitive criticism. His initial strategy, which was meticulously developed by his SHAEF staff well before the D-Day invasion, called for advancing along dual axes, with Montgomery's 21st Army Group in the north and General Omar N. Bradley's 12th Army Group further south. The purpose of these two spearheads was to encircle

Germany's vital Ruhr industrial region, close the pincer east of it, and then advance to the Elbe River, where they would meet westward-advancing Soviets. Eisenhower's strategy was based purely on logistical considerations. He specified that to shorten the supply lines of advancing Allied armies additional ports had to be captured in quick succession to correspond with the drive to the east.

Eisenhower was perfectly willing to amend his plans as the situation evolved and demanded. In August 1944, 58-year-old Lieutenant General Bernard Law Montgomery (he would be promoted to field marshal in September) sent a message to Eisenhower requesting permission to make a concerted thrust to the Elbe River, and then on to Berlin with his mighty 21st Army Group. In Monty's estimation the war would be over in three months if he had his way. He was wrong of course, but he persisted in pressing Eisenhower for his support for this 'single thrust plan', adding that the plains in northern Germany was the terrain that was most conducive to mobile armoured units, and offered the greatest opportunity for a quick victory. Monty went on to say that, in his considered opinion, if he could go on the offensive there, the Germans would have neither the manpower nor the impetus to take him on. It would be the end of the German army. Ike tactfully acknowledged the suggestion but didn't entirely agree with this modus operandi.

Eisenhower was a highly intelligent team player who expertly used his finely-honed skills to manoeuvre and conciliate all parties. He also recognized the importance of allowing General de Gaulle's Free French to be the first Allies to enter Paris. De Gaulle insisted on speciously taking full credit for the liberation of Paris, and in typical De Gaullesque style he made scant reference to the part that the Allies had played. Regardless, SHAEF agreed to de Gaulle's request to lead the French 2nd Division into Paris on point.

Carlton Stauffer, Company G, 2nd Battalion, 12th Infantry Regiment, heard that his regiment would have the honour of being the first US troops to enter Paris. He recalled, 'We were to support the 2nd French Armoured Division, which was given the political role of liberating Paris. To ensure that nothing went awry, the Supreme Headquarters, Allied Expeditionary Forces assigned the responsibility to the 12th Infantry to ensure a smooth liberation. We resumed our motor march some time during the afternoon of the 24th, and since we were in the suburbs of Paris, the celebrating was getting into high gear even then. Madly cheering

The Supreme Commander of the Allied Forces, General of the Army Dwight D. Eisenhower managed to create a powerful, unified military force.

French people wanted our convoy to slow down to give their hands, their flowers, their wine and their sincere thanks to their liberators.

'We all felt an exhilaration that would not be surpassed in the lives of any of us infantrymen. As we entered the Rue d'Italie, our tactical motor march became a huge victory parade, and our vehicles became covered with flowers. The pent-up emotions of four bitter years under the Nazi yoke suddenly burst into wild celebration, and the great French citizens made us feel that each of us was personally responsible for the liberation of these grateful people. We felt wonderful!'

Allied medical units were soon confronted with an emerging problem. Sexually transmitted diseases were becoming rampant among the men. There was little ambiguity regarding their ambitions. For the vast majority it was very simple and according to one GI it was a case of 'don't get killed, just get laid'. The official newspaper of the US armed forces, *Stars and Stripes,* provided useful German phrases for the soldiers such as '*Waffen niederlegen!*' ('Lay down your arms!'). But the recommended French phrases such as 'You have charming eyes,' 'I am not married' and 'Are your parents at home?' appear to have been inspired for one sole purpose. At the time, American propaganda was more geared toward promoting the liberation of Europe as a potential Rabelaisian sexual adventure, rather than a determined quest to free the subjugated people there.

'So we've liberated France more or less, what do we do now?' asked Bill Fitzgerald, Company E, 117th Infantry Regiment. He wouldn't have to wait too long to find out.

US writer Ernest Hemingway was a war correspondent for the American *Collier's* magazine. He arrived in France armed with one almost insatiable purpose. He quickly found his friend Colonel Charles 'Buck' T. Lanham, latched on to the 4th Infantry Division and set out on his personal quest, to liberate the bar of the luxurious Ritz Hotel in Paris. He had a special attachment to the hotel, and particularly to its bar, where he had been known to sink many a charged libation before the war. He said, 'When I dream of afterlife in heaven, the action always takes place in the Paris Ritz.' One exasperated French Resistance fighter said, 'He was obsessed. He did not talk about anything else, except that he wanted to be the first American in Paris to liberate the bar at the Ritz Hotel.' So fervent was Hemingway that he even went as far as arranging a meeting with French General Philippe Leclerc, to request permission to be given enough men to fulfil his personal mission. Leclerc suspiciously raised a Gallic eyebrow, briefly acknowledged Hemingway in the same way one would regard someone recently certified as criminally insane, and flatly refused to acquiesce.

Undeterred, Hemingway commandeered a jeep and a few resistance fighters and on 25 August, dressed in a US army uniform, and full of braggadocio, he arrived at the hotel, on the Place Vendôme. Packing a cocked and loaded Thompson machine gun, he burst into the hotel foyer and announced that he had come to personally liberate it and its bar. The bar had been requisitioned in June 1940 by the Nazis and occupied by German dignitaries, including Hermann Goering and Joseph Goebbels. Slightly mystified by this unexpected intrusion, hotel manager Claude Auzello cautiously approached Hemingway, but before he could get within a few feet Hemingway bellowed, 'Where are the Germans? I have come to liberate the Ritz.' 'Monsieur,' replied the manager dryly, 'they left a long time ago, and I cannot let you enter with a weapon.' Hemingway looked at the gun, and then scanned the bar. No contest. He threw the gun in the back of the stationary jeep and quickly returned to the bar where he sank no fewer than 51 Dry Martinis before moving on.

While Hemingway was single-handedly liberating Paris, Monty was presenting a new plan to US General Omar Bradley in an attempt to coerce his support. The plan entailed the US 12th Army and the British 21st Army remaining together as a solid mass of some 40 divisions, which would, in Monty's myopic view, 'be so strong that it need fear nothing'. The combined armies would advance north-eastwards to clear the Channel coast, ultimately securing Antwerp and south Holland en route, and then head east to Aachen and Cologne. The whole movement would pivot on Paris. The object would be, according to one of Monty's men, 'to establish a powerful air force in Belgium, to secure bridgeheads over the Rhine before the winter began, and to seize the Ruhr as quickly as possible'. Bradley appeared to be in complete agreement with this outline plan, in principle at least, but he would later demonstrate his capacity to be duplicitous. At that time Bradley and his 12th Army Group were reluctantly subject to Monty's operational control. It was the first time Bradley would deceive Montgomery. It wouldn't be the last.

Lofty Field Marshal Sir Alan Brooke, 1st Viscount Alanbrooke, who had scant regard for Eisenhower's military acumen, had inspired Monty's suggested strategy. Eisenhower felt that the risks involved with this single thrust strategy were far too great to consider at that juncture. Monty refused to be assuaged and remained characteristically intransigent. He wanted to lead the charge, be the all-conquering hero and be provided with the necessary supplies to accomplish this, even if it was to the detriment of other Allied commanders in the field. He had already proven that he could be magnanimous in victory, and now he was again hungry for glory.

Monty was bitterly disappointed when his plan was ultimately rejected, but as a subordinate to the Supreme Commander he had little option than to obey. This caused a rift between Eisenhower and Monty that never completely healed. For months there had been murmurs of discontent regarding Eisenhower's leadership, emanating primarily from Alanbrooke. Eisenhower, as always, ignored his detractors. Alanbrooke suggested installing a ground forces commander (preferably Monty), claiming that, 'National parochialism is impeding the optimal operational command structure and strategy.'

Eisenhower expertly deflected this potential slight and simply carried on with his job. He convened a meeting at SHAEF HQ and presented his plan. The mission of securing the approaches to Antwerp or Rotterdam and capturing additional Channel ports would be allocated to Monty's 21st Army Group. Lt. Gen. Omar N. Bradley's 12th Army Group was to reduce the French port of Brest as soon as possible and link up with the 6th US Army Group under the talented General Jacob L. Devers, who was rapidly advancing from the south.

Devers had participated in Operation Dragoon, 15 August 1944, in southern France, which was derisively referred to by the units that had fought in Normandy as 'The Champagne Campaign'. The Allies down there had defeated seven German divisions on the first day and advanced almost 200 km (124 miles) in one week. Eisenhower's strategy would facilitate support of the 12th Army Group by providing assistance from Allied units that had landed in the south of France. He had opted for a broad front strategy that would be operable once adequate logistic support was ensured. He would later demonstrate that he was flexible, or rather perfectly capable of having his opinion swayed under duress. Meanwhile there was discontent among some Allied generals.

Monty had made laboriously slow progress leading up to and during the breakout from Normandy. He was a prudent general who liked to know that the odds were in his favour before launching any attack. This

Bernard Montgomery, affectionately known as 'Monty', was often at odds with Eisenhower.

was probably due to his experiences in World War I. He heavily criticized Great War generals, such as Douglas Haig, because of their apparent indifference to casualty figures. Monty later commented, 'the frightful casualties appalled me. The so-called "good fighting generals" of the war appeared to me to be those who had a complete disregard for human life'.

One of Monty's harshest critics was Eisenhower's Chief of Staff, Walter 'Beetle' Bedell Smith who, according to one fellow officer, 'had all the charm of a rattlesnake'. General Omar Bradley and 3rd Army commander General George S. Patton also complained vociferously that Monty was too slow and over-cautious. Patton once even described Monty as a 'tired old fart'. While the commanders were casting these aspersions other, more pressing, problems were developing.

During the last week of August supply difficulties reached critical proportions. The rapid Allied advance across France and north into Belgium had occurred with such speed that it caused some terrible logistical problems. Supplying an army on the move was a colossal task. The million gallons of gasoline and 1,815 tonnes (2,000 tons) of artillery ammunition used daily were still being transported by road from Cherbourg harbour. Almost 95 per cent of all supplies shipped to France remained stacked upon wharves and beaches far to the rear, awaiting transport.

In an attempt to tackle the situation, on 25 August 1944 the 'Red Ball Express' was conceived. Logisticians from across the ETO (European Theatre of Operations) pooled all available truck assets and created transportation trucking units for one sole purpose, to supply the armies on the move. The term 'Red Ball' was a common railway phrase used in America in the 1940s that simply meant express mail. The Red Ball Express drivers would head out on one-way supply routes, which were specifically allocated to optimize logistics distribution. In the first month, the express delivered 263,000 tonnes (290,000 tons) of supplies to the front. At its peak, the operation employed 23,000 men using almost 6,000 vehicles that operated around the clock. African-Americans consti-tuted around 75 per cent of the truck drivers who kept the Red Ball rolling, and also served as mechanics. John Houston (the father of singer Whitney Houston) once said, 'I remember falling asleep on top of a jeep hood when it was raining like hell. I didn't know the difference.'

In the twilight hours while infinite black skies were still dusted with stars, truck engines coughed lethargically into life and set out from their base. They were going to make a round trip on a continuous merry-go-round along roads fraught with danger and potential demise. It was a 24/7 production line churning out truck after truck. When the autumn rains came the roads would be transformed into barely traversable quagmires that often rendered vehicles immobile. Drivers would work frantically to get their trucks back on the road because they knew that while they weren't moving they were vulnerable to the enemy and anything could happen. Red Ball Express driver Arthur Joseph Jr. vividly recalled his service, 'The driver was at the wheel and ready to transport us. The trucks rolled off into deep water, floating. The trucks had wax over the wires to protect the motor and ensure that the trucks did not stop. There was water in our two-and-a-half-ton trucks up to our necks. Everybody made it. We were well trained. We drove trucks only; we did not load them. Our greatest fear was fighter planes. Fighter planes would eat you up. They could come at you from out of nowhere. We were strafed many times, always by a single plane.

'When the plane came, you didn't get off the highway. As long as you stayed on the highway, you were all right. Now the next problem we had was going through this rural town where the roads are so narrow that German sympathizers might throw something inside of the truck. Going through a small town, they would sometimes stop the lead truck or they might hit the back truck. But if they hit the front truck, that caused the trucks to stop and they could have a field day. There were also snipers. Every truck had a fifty-caliber machine gun. We made our runs both night and day. Night was all right, but you had to drive with no lights on. No lights. You really had to know where the road was. So, night driving was a terrible job, but it was also safe because of the "cat eyes" [military driving lights]. But once you used the tail light, you could be in big trouble.'

These were the men of the Red Ball Express.

In late August Eisenhower held another staff meeting. This time he wanted to discuss the future conduct of the war. A decision was made to revise the system of command, a move that was in all probability inspired by Alanbrooke's 'Ground Commander' suggestion. Eisenhower decided to take personal command of all the army groups, simply because he had the authority to do so. He also wanted to definitively address Monty's 'single thrust' plan and was aware that he'd already presented this to Bradley. Eisenhower decided to completely ignore it and dispatch Bradley's 12th Army Group toward Metz and the Saar River. Monty strongly disagreed with these proposals, as expected, and a few days later he approached Bradley again. This time Monty left the meeting exasperated that Bradley had made a complete about turn on the matter, and switched allegiances to Bradley's long-time friend and West Point roomy Eisenhower, who remained insistent that the main effort of the 12th Army Group should be directed eastward.

Monty once remarked, 'Eisenhower is a nice chap, but no soldier.' General Patton, who held divergent opinions on just about everything regarding Monty, had also said something to that effect. Many years later during an interview with *The Longest Day* author Cornelius Ryan, Eisenhower said of Monty, 'First of all he's a psychopath. Don't forget that.' Psychopath is a bit harsh, but according to historian Anthony Beevor, Field Marshal Montgomery's 'high-handed' approach to his superiors and 'strange' behaviour may indeed have been an indication he had Asperger's syndrome. Contemporary psychiatrists may have even placed Monty on the autism spectrum, but historians should stick to history. There's no doubt that Monty could be self-aggrandizing and opinionated and he could indeed be described as a socially inept loner. Not known for reserving his opinions, Monty was adored by the British press and British troops, even if he didn't particularly endear himself to other contemporaries, especially Eisenhower, whom he often badgered to the point of exasperation.

An exchange concerning Monty between Prime Minister Churchill and King George VI at Windsor shows the strong opinions he provoked. Churchill was the grandson of the 7th Duke of Marlborough, born at Blenheim Palace in Oxfordshire and considered by King George VI, and many others, to be a genuine member of the British aristocracy. He had a great rapport with the king. 'Monty was here a few days ago,' said the monarch as he languidly drew on a cigarette. Churchill thought that Monty harboured political aspirations. 'I think Monty is after my job,' Churchill said to his Highness. 'Thank God for that Winston. I thought he was after mine,' replied the King.

Meanwhile V-1 rockets, launched from northern France and Belgium, were devastating London. Churchill called Eisenhower to ask him if he could attack the V-1 bases. On 23 August 1944 Eisenhower placed the entire Allied Airborne Army (US 82nd and 101st Divisions and British

A soldier waves on a Red Ball Express convoy. These were at the heart of the Allied supply chains in Europe from August 1944 onwards.

1st and Polish Brigade) under Monty's command and acquiesced to his plan to strike for the Ruhr, on the condition that Monty knock out the V-1 sites and take Antwerp en route.

By 8 September Field Marshal Montgomery had taken the V-1 launch sites, along with the Belgian cities of Brussels and Antwerp. He'd taken Antwerp with the docks relatively undamaged, intact but completely useless because as long as the Germans held the mouth of the Scheldt River no Allied shipping would be able to enter the harbour. By then German V-2 rockets were striking London from sites in Holland and Denmark. The first V-2 was launched against Paris on 6 September 1944. Two days later, the first of more than 1,100 V-2s was launched against the United Kingdom. Belgium was also heavily bombarded. Tracking V-2 targets was more difficult for the Allies because they were launched from mobile platforms and the missile had a maximum range of roughly 250 km (155 miles). One British witness to the effects of a V-2 attack said, 'A V-2 rocket landed, killing 23 people. When I arrived, there was a crater 200 ft wide and 200 ft deep, with water mains pouring, and gas mains burning, and surrounding houses destroyed.'

While Monty toed the line with Eisenhower's strategy of creating a 'broad front' to drive back German forces into Germany, he remained resolute in his conviction regarding the potential efficacy of a concentrated assault. On the strength of this he proposed Operation Market Garden. It was a daring plan using the Airborne Army to seize bridges in Holland at Eindhoven, Nijmegen and Arnhem. British 30 Corps would link up with the Airborne and the way would be open to Berlin. The operation didn't go exactly to plan. Monty claimed to have created a salient into the German line, but it was in fact an impractical cul-de-sac that subjected two US airborne units and British ground troops to subsequent weeks of hard combat. Even if the British 1st Airborne had taken Arnhem, it is highly doubtful that they would have been able to turn east and head into the heart of the Third Reich.

Despite the failure of Operation Market Garden to achieve all its objectives, Montgomery remained in a strident mood. Finally, he turned his attention to the opening of Antwerp's port when he said, 'It is now absolutely essential before we can advance deep into Germany.' Up until that juncture he hadn't regarded the opening of the Scheldt estuary as an immediate priority due to his other distractions, but now, finally, he understood that it was an imperative and in retrospect this should have preceded and taken full priority over the wasteful airborne operation.

Monty expertly deflected blame for the failure of Market Garden claiming that it had been a 90 per cent success. Paratroopers such as Arthur Letchford, Company C, 2nd Battalion, 1st British Para, was inclined to disagree with that statistic when he said, 'For me and my brother it was a 100 per cent bloody failure, we spent the rest of the war in a Stalag.'

In his official report after Market Garden, 1st Airborne Division commander Major General R. E. Urquhart wrote: 'The operation was not 100 per cent successful and did not quite end as we had intended. The losses were heavy but all ranks appreciate that the risks involved were reasonable. There is no doubt that all would willingly undertake another operation under similar conditions in the future. We have no regrets.' From the original 10,000 British paratroopers, Urquhart was one of the 2,163 that made it out. It was a very stoic and British response reminiscent of the British cavalry who survived the charge of the Light Brigade: 'Can we go again, sir?'

Nevertheless, it was Lieutenant-General Frederick 'Boy' Browning who briefed Monty on the situation and repeatedly dismissed the available intelligence. Furthermore, it was Eisenhower who placed the whole Allied Airborne Army under Monty's command, along with sanctioning the operation and giving permission for it to go ahead, despite clamorous protests from other Allied commanders, including General George S. Patton, who wanted to sequester additional supplies for his own drive to the Rhine. Just for the record, it's a widely held military myth that fierce competition existed between Monty and Patton. Monty was too far up the pecking order and was too arrogant to seriously consider any opinions the pugnacious American general had, and he had many.

Although the capture of Antwerp hadn't been entirely successful regarding the use of the harbour, it had seriously compromised three corps (67th, 86th and 89th) of the German 15th Army, which was ensconced in a potentially precarious situation west of the city and south of the Scheldt River. On the day Antwerp fell, a German general noted in his diary that: 'The British advance on Antwerp had in effect encircled General von Zangen's 15th Army.'

An opportunity was squandered here because an Allied push to Breda to the north of Antwerp and just over the Belgian–Dutch border would have severed the 15th Army's escape route across the Scheldt by way of

Walcheren and South Beveland. Unfortunately, military inertia on the Allied side in Antwerp was rampant at the time, and there were other distractions, which allowed the 15th Army to escape relatively unimpeded. They lived to fight another day and would re-appear later in the year.

While most of France, Luxembourg and Belgium were returning to some semblance of normality, this wasn't the case in the Netherlands. In the autumn of 1944, the southern part of the Netherlands may have been liberated, as far as the Rhine River, but the northern and eastern part of the country remained strictly under German control. After the failure of Market Garden, the Germans implemented a range of draconian measures on the Dutch. Arnhem was destroyed beyond all recognition and its people were evacuated. All food transports were restricted for six weeks and the movement of coal from the liberated south also ceased. Gas and electricity supplies were disconnected. People chopped down trees and dismantled empty houses to get fuel. The amount of food available on ration began to steadily decrease. Soon the effects began to result in terrible suffering for the population. Combining this with the damage done to the Dutch railway network in preparation for the invasion, and the general shortage of agricultural products, it caused what became known in Dutch popular culture as the 'Hunger Winter' of 1944–45. Roughly 20,000 Dutch men and women perished as a result of this cruel Nazi-made famine.

While the Allies prepared to settle in for the winter and make preparations for a new offensive to commence in the New Year, the Germans had other plans. The ensuing Battle of the Bulge would go down in history as the largest land battle in United States military history and one of the most monumental battles of World War II.

CHAPTER TWO

Reliable intelligence

MANY HISTORIANS HAVE REFERRED TO 'Allied intelligence' leading up to the Battle of the Bulge as if it was a contradiction in terms. There are few subjects that have the capacity to induce such a polarity of opinion. So many decades have passed since the battle that allocation of blame, if blame could be attributed, is now of little or no consequence. But it's always interesting to re-assess. Intelligence reports were disseminated prodigiously to all Allied intelligence departments for the duration, but not always closely analysed.

It is estimated that between October and January 1944, over 11,000 German messages were intercepted. This amounted to between 40 and 50 ULTRA* intercepts every day. ULTRA was not an acronym. The name simply referred to an innovative British invention that was used to crack the famed Enigma Code. This was achieved mainly thanks to the work

---

* The Bletchley solutions were widely known under the collective name of ULTRA. Eisenhower told the administrative chief of Bletchley: 'The intelligence which has emanated from you... has been of priceless value to me.'

of the much-maligned genius Alan Turing and many others (mostly women) who worked at Bletchley Park. Details about the Enigma Code were strictly concealed under pain of death from the Germans to allow messages to continue to be intercepted. The ULTRA programme that cracked Enigma was a massive collaborative effort that entailed and engaged a veritable cast of hundreds.

By autumn 1944, Bletchley's highly capable staff was only managing to read around 20 per cent of Wehrmacht communications. However, many decoded messages from all sources were often deciphered and translated too slowly to impact events on the battlefield. There were still around 100,000 Enigma machines operative by members of the Third Reich, and although some of the messages were little more than insignificant conversions of German abbreviations, the staff at Bletchley Park forwarded each decoded message by a secure radio and teleprinter network to the relevant military headquarters. The information they collected, and the means by which it was collected, was so sensitive that the secret of Enigma wasn't made public until 1974.

SHAEF had attempted to cover all the bases regarding intelligence. Inter-Allied committees dealt with most of this work. The remit for the committees also incorporated censorship, intelligence, psychological warfare, displaced persons and counter-intelligence, and even included forestry and timber supply along with communications, POWs and radio broadcasts.

From 1944 onwards three American detachments were assigned by SHAEF to work with the British intelligence gathering services at Bletchley Park. This marked the beginning of the sharing of high-level decrypted German communications traffic between Britain and the US. The information SHAEF's G-2 intelligence office issued in its weekly reviews generally reflected reports received from the Intelligence Divisions at both Army and Army Group-levels. These summaries incorporated additional information obtained from the British Red Cross and other sources. There were restrictions because not all intelligence could be conveyed for fear of endangering or revealing their sources. Specific and frequently highly reliable information provided by ULTRA would rarely, if ever, be included in SHAEF weekly summaries.

For armies in the field there were numerous other ways of gathering intelligence, such as patrol reports, radio intercepts, signals traffic analysis, prisoners-of-war, civilian and refugee interrogations, assess-

ments of captured letters and documents, interpretation of aerial photo-
graphs and artillery sound-ranging. In military Command Posts (CPs)
G-2 personnel (staff of the American military intelligence), polyglots and
prisoner interrogation teams assessed and disseminated most of the
information gleaned from the sources. Another prime source of information on enemy activity was accumulated by aerial photography, but
this was severely hampered during the autumn and winter months in
Europe when mist and low cloud covered most of the landscape,
rendering this method temporarily obsolete.

The gathering of reliable intelligence outside the ULTRA network was
a spurious and perilous game. A former British secret service agent who
worked during the war said, 'Intelligence work necessarily involves such
cheating, lying and betraying that it has a deleterious effect on the character.
I never met anyone professionally engaged in it whom I should care to
trust in any capacity.' That applied pretty much across the board. However,
ULTRA was generally regarded as being highly dependable. By 1944, ULTRA
was making a difference, but it was accompanied by the complacency that
caused one of the greatest intelligence fiascos of the whole war.

Bradley noted in his autobiography, 'One major fault on our side was
that our intelligence community had come to rely far too heavily on
ULTRA to the exclusion of other intelligence sources.' By December 1944
Bradley's 12th Army Group was one of the largest US ground combat
forces ever created. Inside Bradley's HQ, the Appreciation Group operated
an 'ULTRA room' which received and assembled Bletchley material with
other sources to provide estimates of German army numbers and dispositions. The 12th Army Group held two daily ULTRA briefings, both of
which would have been attended by Bradley. The intelligence that ULTRA
provided was considered so sensitive that the data provided by Bletchley
was forbidden from inclusion in Allied written intelligence reports or
summaries.

Another problem was that the Germans were so convinced of the
infallibility of their codes that they had no concept that they could have
been breached, but there were dissenters. When German U-boats were
tracked down in obscure locations, Admiral Doenitz suspected that
German messages were being intercepted but didn't take any action to
have his suspicions denied or confirmed.

The Allies had the capacity to be incredibly inventive to the point of
ingenuity when passing false information to the Germans. One particular

unit became masters of deception during the autumn of 1944. In September 1944 the country of Luxembourg was haunted. It unsuspectingly played host to an Allied tactical deception unit known as the Ghost Army. Psychological warfare played an integral part on all sides in World War II. Its purpose was to circulate half-truths, lies and rumours by all available media. The 1,100 men of the 23rd Headquarters Special Troops formed a strictly clandestine unit that operated with the utmost secrecy. They were experts in deception and their activities remained classified for almost 36 years after the end of the war. This unit was unlike any other. It was a peculiar collective of highly-skilled artists and craftsmen recruited mainly from north-eastern art schools whose sole purpose was to deceive and confuse the enemy.

Using inflatable tanks and other vehicles, the Ghost Army had successfully misled the Nazis into thinking that the June 1944 invasion would come from Dover. During the war they devised many ingenious means to fox the enemy, such as fake convoys, phantom divisions and even ersatz headquarters. On many occasions they successfully conned the German army into thinking certain US divisions were present or in proximity, when they were absolutely nowhere near.

The purpose of the Ghost Army was to sow the seeds of chaos and disorder among the Axis forces. They used much more than simple visual props to achieve the deception. They also used something they referred to as 'sonic deception'. Assisted by engineers at Bell Labs, a team from the unit's 3132 Signal Service Company Special travelled to Fort Knox to record sounds of armoured and infantry units on to cutting-edge wire recorders (the predecessors to tape recorders). Then they created complex audio mixes compiled from sounds that matched the atmosphere they wanted to create. These sounds would be broadcast from powerful amplifiers and speakers that were mounted on half-tracks. This combination proved to be so effective that the sounds could be heard up to 20 km (12 miles) away. It was in effect a forerunner of psychological warfare. They even orchestrated 'fake news' radio broadcasts, long before it became a popular contemporary expression. These radio broadcasts were so convincing they even fooled the US-born Nazi propagandist radio broadcaster Mildred Gillars, known to the Allies as 'Axis Sally', into thinking that certain Allied units were in certain areas.

While General Patton was massing his forces around the French town of Metz in preparation for an attack, the Ghost Army were donning the insignia and emblems of the 6th Armored Division. In his haste to reach Metz, Patton had inadvertently left a potentially precarious 113 km (70 mile) gap in his line on his north-eastern flank. At that time there was only a smattering of US troops belonging to the 3rd Cavalry Group covering the whole region.

When the call came though the 23rd Headquarters Special Troops raced 300 km (186 miles) across France in an attempt to remedy the situation. Aware that certain German units were in proximity, for four straight nights they deployed 'sonic' trucks to project the sound of a division assembling. The deception proved to be so convincing that a colonel from the US 3rd Cavalry approached some of the Ghost Army men to ask what was going on. They explained that they were only broadcasting pre-recorded sounds of tanks, but the colonel was difficult to assuage. He could hear tanks and that was good enough for him. It took a while to calm the man down and fully explain the situation. Meanwhile, some of the men wearing 6th Armored insignia began infiltrating nearby towns and villages to add more credence to the ruse.

They even went as far as dressing some of their soldiers in Military Police uniforms adorned with 6th Armored patches, and placing them at intersections along the route. The whole escapade became known as Operation Bettembourg and proved to be another resounding success for the Ghost Army, who remained operative for the duration of World War II.

In September 1944, Operation Market Garden had highlighted the importance of failing to act on reliable intelligence. The same problem confronted the first American patrols when they surveyed and crossed the German border in the same month. Allied intelligence on the Siegfried line, known in Germany as the 'West Wall', was at best vague, at worst almost non-existent. Most available intelligence predated 1940, and advancing US units discovered to their detriment that four long years had provided herbaceous camouflage for many of the bunkers and pillboxes there. Moreover, aerial recon that had worked so well in the hedgerows of Normandy now failed to zero many enemy positions. Many soldiers among the rank and file of the advancing Allies asked, 'Where are these old German men and pre-pubescent youths we've been told about?'

Intelligence reports made little impact on the soldiers doing the actual fighting. As the 30th US Infantry approached the German border via Belgium and the Netherlands, Frank Towers, Company M, 120th

Regiment, 30th Division, said, 'While we were in Belgium I saw many Belgian people shame the men and women who had collaborated with the Germans. They required the women who had been consorting with the Germans to strip down naked. They would shave their heads and paint swastikas on their bodies, then would march them down the main street. It was quite a sight. It gave us a laugh to see these naked women being whipped down the street by the Belgian people (who took it very seriously, because these women had consorted with German officers). They were just giving them some payback.'

While the Allies were heading towards Germany, Frank had seen first-hand the terrible retribution exacted on French women who had been accused of 'collaboration horizontale'. They were frog-marched into public places and humiliated by having their heads shaved. The practice of head shaving became ubiquitous during the liberation euphoria in France in 1944. The trend would extend to Belgium, Luxembourg and the Netherlands during the ensuing months. It didn't appear to matter that many of the head-shaving perpetrators were not even members of the Resistance. It was even suspected and later confirmed that quite a few of them had even been petty collaborators themselves, and had sought to divert attention from their own lack of Resistance credentials. A strong element of exhibitionism and vicarious eroticism evolved among the tondeurs ('head shavers') and their enthusiastic crowd, even though the punishment in fact symbolized if anything the de-sexualization of their victim. It was a public display to appease the masses not unlike those gatherings before the guillotine 150 years previously.

George Schneider of HQ Company, 120th Regiment, 30th US Infantry Division, had also seen these public humiliations but was more preoccupied with reaching the German frontier. He wrote: 'The Siegfried Line was now only 25 kilometers to the east. This was Germany's western wall of defense and was heavily fortified with pillboxes and rows of dragon's teeth snaking along the border. These dragon's teeth were reinforced concrete, angular pillars in columns two and three deep for the purpose of stopping tanks and other vehicles.'

Most of Belgium had been liberated during the first few weeks of September before the Allies reached the frontiers of the Third Reich. By the time the 30th Division arrived over four-fifths of the Belgian population were suffering from vitamin deficiency-related conditions such as rickets and scurvy, although this was more prevalent in the north and industrial areas where food was incredibly scarce. This was less so in the Ardennes region due to the ingenious hoarding of the residents and the rich agricultural pastures there. One veterinarian who lived in Bastogne was completely unaffected by German requisitions of food and livestock and kept his whole family and innumerable relatives supplied with quality meat and vegetables for the duration of World War II. His daughter whom he had brought home to Belgium after his service in the Belgian Congo was a nurse who worked in the north, but she would get to taste the delights of delectable Ardennes cuisine when she returned home. She was due to arrive on 16 December, in time for Christmas. Her name was Augusta Chiwy and she wouldn't be recognized for her heroic actions until 70 years after the fact.

The occupying German forces had imposed a system whereby a significant percentage of food stocks was requisitioned for their war effort. In addition to this, by 1944 Belgians had suffered the consequences of an economic blockade established by the Allies, which prevented all free trade. In direct response to the draconian measures imposed on the population by the German authorities, some individuals in the Ardennes engaged in the illegal cultivation of food and clandestine rearing of animals for personal consumption. It was generally accepted that life was considerably better for residents of rural areas as opposed to the lives of city dwellers, whose only recourse was often provided by the thriving black market. This led to an influx of young people from cities and industrial areas offering their services as farm labourers in the Ardennes and Luxembourg.

Furthermore, numerous monasteries and convents in the area cultivated their own vegetables and kept their own livestock. The Germans were aware of the fact that, in addition to the Belgian authorities, the Catholic Church was a powerful player on the socio-political field so they were often reluctant to tamper with the equilibrium. The extensive and antiquated organizational powers regarding congregations and Catholic education were the primary sources of power in Belgium and the German authorities were wary. Nazi policies in Belgium were inevitably influenced by the Vatican, which just happened to be in a country that had been a sworn ally until 25 July 1943, when Mussolini had been removed from office and arrested by King Victor Emmanuel III.

On 25 September ULTRA decoded a message sent between German commanders a week earlier. It stated emphatically that all SS units on the Western Front must be withdrawn and assigned to a new 6th Panzer Army. General Edwin L. Sibert, Assistant Chief of Staff (G-2) of General Omar Bradley's 12th Army Group, had mentioned the possibility that the German 6th Panzer Army could be employed in a counter-attacking role. He later detracted from his statement by writing, 'While it is likely Rundstedt would employ a part or all of the 6th Panzer Army in a counter-attack against any bridgeheads east of the Roer River, in conjunction with flooding the river, in order to protect the Cologne corridor, it seems unlikely that he would bring them westward across the Roer to commit them in a major counter-offensive.'

From October 1944 the Allies began encountering disconcerting levels of German resistance as their armies began to extend tentacles deeper into the heart of the German Reich. Allied intelligence services came under pressure to produce the goods. By late autumn torrential rain that had inundated and beset the Allied armies in the western theatre was beginning to turn to sleet and snow causing temperatures to dip below freezing along the whole Allied line. The vicious fighting that had occurred in the Hürtgen Forest had dissipated, and for some inexplicable reason the Germans had cleared out, and no one had questioned why.

Down in the vicinity of Metz through most of November as part of Patton's 3rd Army, the 10th Armored Division had been on the offensive. They had braved incessant autumnal rains and crossed the Moselle River at Malling, then driven over to the Saar River, north of Metz. Their battles around Metz had introduced them to the debilitating weather-related health problems that could arise from having to endure low temperatures and almost constant wet weather over long periods. Trench foot and hypothermia was the cause of many casualties. The other recurring problem that had initially reared its ugly head after the liberation of Paris was STDs. As the Allies pushed north some American units remained in France. That September in 1944 General Charles Gerhardt was commanding the 29th Infantry Division as it rolled through Brittany. Gerhardt decided that there was no other way to assuage the passions of his division; his boys needed sex and they would get it. He ordered his chief of staff to open a brothel. The local civil affairs officer, Asa Gardiner, managed to coerce the local police force into giving up the name of a pimp named Morot. The pimp, in turn, recommended four prostitutes who were residing in proximity to the American division.

A nearby house was requisitioned and Gerhardt approved the sign for the establishment, which read 'Blue and Gray Corral, Riding Lessons 100 Francs.' When the Corral opened for business on 10 September, 21 GIs, transported by jeep from the bivouac area, waited patiently in line. After only five hours of brisk business, the brothel was shut down on the orders of the division chaplain, on the grounds that such a place of ill repute incited moral corruption. General George Patton didn't agree – he had the opinion that sexual fulfilment was necessary for male physical vigour. When he heard about the activities he said, 'If they don't fuck, they don't fight.'

After a rain-drenched November in the Alsace-Lorraine region of France, sickness in the army was rampant. One division in Patton's 3rd Army reported over 3,000 severe cases of trench foot, but this would prove to be only a small taste of what was to come. The men of the 10th were currently taking a short break prior to preparing for the 3rd Army drive to the Rhine, but that wouldn't happen in the near future. A soldier in the 10th Armored Division complained about the weather conditions around Metz. 'Everyone was soaked to the skin and we never completely dried out. Sleeping with your socks under your armpits helped a little but the constant rain had saturated every single item of clothing we had. According to some reports it was the wettest November in living memory, but you know what happens when you think things can't get any worse?'

Meanwhile, in early November, at Bletchley Park in England, suspicions were aroused when ULTRA cryptanalysts succeeded in deciphering the *Reichsbahn* (German railway) codes, which clearly indicated that around 800 trains had been requisitioned by the German army for the purpose of transporting men and equipment to the west. They also intercepted messages concerning the significant relocation of Luftwaffe forces. This information was duly dispatched to SHAEF and ETO, but at that time there were few officers there who believed that the Germans had either the manpower or the means to seriously launch a major offensive in the west.

In the autumn months of September, October and November, although estimates vary, it is assumed that the Allies incurred around 56,000 battle casualties. As daunting as that number is, it pales by comparison with Russian casualties. During the opening months of the Soviet army's Operation Bagration, while making their 640 km drive (400 miles) from

General George S. Patton, Commander of the US 3rd Army wearing his lieutenant general uniform.

Vitebsk to Warsaw's outskirts, the Soviets suffered 178,000 killed or missing and 590,848 wounded. One of the reasons why the Soviet army sustained so many casualties was their often deplorable and highly questionable military tactics.

The strategy and tactics employed by east and west differed substantially. Anglo-American generals used tactics that aimed to encircle and capture their adversary. In the east the Red Army frequently employed almost suicidal frontal attacks hammered home with brute force that didn't stop short of annihilation.

23 November 1944. ULTRA intercepts indicated that remaining German air forces were being moved west and had been ordered to protect large troop movements into the Eifel region. Montgomery's 21st Army Group G-2 (or intelligence officer), Brigadier Williams, stated emphatically that, 'there was no need for worry about any possible German initiative, because Hitler's forces were in an advanced state of erosion'. Keep calm and carry on, as long as one has good intelligence.

General Sibert had dismissively acknowledged the possibility of a German attack but assumed that, if it came, it would probably occur during the Allied planned crossing of the Roer River. He wasn't above embellishing his intelligence reports either, on the basis that he assumed that nobody read them anyway. In his report written during the first weeks of December he appeared to be predicting the imminent capitulation of German forces when he stated, 'With continued Allied pressure in the south and in the north, the breaking point may develop suddenly and without warning.' Sibert told one soldier that he had decided to make the reports a little more exciting to read by employing the talents of Major Ralph Ingersoll, a well-known editorial writer. Ingersoll thought long and hard on the matter before he wrote his contribution to the Allied war effort with the largely forgettable words, 'The enemy has had it.'

In November 1944, British Major General Kenneth Strong was working as Eisenhower's personal G-2. It was a good appointment because Strong knew the Germans well. He had served as assistant military attaché in Berlin shortly before the outbreak of war in 1939. In February 1943 he was appointed G-2 of Allied Force Headquarters in the Mediterranean and had assisted in armistice negotiations with the Italians. In the spring of 1944 he was appointed G-2 of SHAEF. Monty once unflatteringly described Strong as 'a chinless horror'. On one occasion Strong reported in his weekly intelligence summary, 'The intentions of the enemy in the Aachen sector, therefore, become quite clear. He [the enemy] is fighting the main battle with his infantry formations and army Panzer divisions, and with these he hopes to blunt our offensive. Meanwhile, 6th SS Panzer Army waits behind the Roer River, either to continue the defensive action, and prevent bridgeheads from being established, or, if Rundstedt gauges that we are becoming exhausted, to counter-attack and regain lost ground.' At the beginning of December Strong had noticed that some German Panzer divisions were being removed from the front lines and that there appeared to be more *Volksgrenadier* divisions in the Eifel region than what was required to maintain a static front, but he didn't regard this as a reason for consternation.

Strong had mentioned the existence of the new 6th Panzer Army, adding that the 5th Panzer Army had somehow disappeared from the line in the Alsace-Lorraine region where Patton was based with his 3rd Army. Patton had also remarked to his G-2, Colonel Koch, that the Germans had failed to follow their own doctrine and standard practice of counter-attacking against 3rd Army operations in the Saar region, despite the fact that there were reportedly German forces available there. What on earth was going on? Despite indications to the contrary, Allied intelligence still predicated all their estimates on the expected early collapse of the German war effort, despite the fact that it was becoming overtly apparent that the Germans were up to something.

By 14 December, the Allies' G-2 intelligence unit's war maps still indicated only four German divisions opposite General Troy Middleton's VIII Corps, with two Panzer divisions positioned to the rear of this area, apparently in the process of moving north. Bradley's former command, US 1st Army, had its HQ at the art nouveau Hôtel Britannique in the fashionable Ardennes town of Spa, where 1st Army G-2 Colonel Benjamin A. ('Monk') Dickson, an unequivocal, uncompromising 1918 graduate of West Point with an engineering degree from MIT, was, owing to his language skills in French and German, working in intelligence. He personally presented the Bletchley material to General Courtney Hodges and his chief of staff who analysed reports that arrived regarding the Ardennes region of Belgium. Dickson wasted no time in expressing his consternation regarding an ostensible accumulation of enemy forces to the east of the Ardennes. He had been contemplating the prospect of a

German attack since early November but incorrectly indicated that the Germans appeared to be preparing to attack the British and the 9th Army from above Aachen in the direction of Venlo in the Netherlands. He added that the probability of an attack against General Courtney Hodges' 1st Army was negligible. Dickson wasn't taken seriously by his colleagues and was subsequently ordered to take some overdue furlough in Paris.

Meanwhile G-2 intelligence assistant chief, Major General Kenneth Strong, had received additional intelligence concerning significant enemy troop movements. According to his information, during the first week of December no fewer than nine Panzer divisions had been removed from the Eastern Front and re-allocated to the west. Based on his findings Strong dispatched a summary to the senior Allied commanders, stating his belief that the Belgian Ardennes was potentially the location of an impending German counter-offensive. Eisenhower acknowledged this report and expressed enough concern to send Strong to General Omar Bradley's headquarters to discuss the possibility of a German attack in the Ardennes. Bradley was completely dismissive. 'Let them come,' he said. He was preoccupied with the concern that his 12th Army group was again going to be placed under Monty, who had written to Eisenhower asking for permission to launch an attack north of the Ruhr.

Eisenhower suggested positioning both the 21st and the 12th Armies north of the Ardennes, and placing Bradley under Monty's operational command to achieve the objective. Monty sent a further message to Eisenhower stating, 'Bradley and I together are a good team. We worked together in Normandy, under you, and we won a great victory. Things have not been so good since you separated us.' That was putting it mildly because, by this stage of the war, Bradley saw things quite differently and he had made clear his opinions about Monty to Eisenhower on a number of occasions.

By 28 November 1944 the Allied supply lines had been reduced thanks to the Canadian army effort in securing the Walcheren peninsula, so that shipping could finally reach the Belgian port of Antwerp. Up until that juncture Allied commanders in the field had suffered almost insurmountable logistics problems. Bill Davis, of the Black Watch, Royal Highland Regiment Canada, was there and experienced the action firsthand. He said, 'After we fought our way out of Antwerp, we were given the job of sealing off the bottom of this peninsula and by taking a town called Woensdrecht, which sat at the very neck of the peninsula. That was one of the occasions when the order came down from up above, that this was how we do it and no ifs, ands or buts, just do it.'

Canadian units had cleared out the Walcheren peninsula and effectively opened the estuary to allow Allied shipping to reach Antwerp. The first convoy led by the Canadian-built freighter *Fort Cataraqui* entered the harbour and Antwerp was once again open for business. New supply routes could be established for the Allied efforts in the north and provide vital fuel and provisions for the Allied advance to liberate Europe, but there was still work to be done. It wasn't over yet.

Meanwhile, ULTRA provided further information regarding the movement of German troops and armaments to the region bordering the Belgian Ardennes; unfortunately, these reports were treated with incredulity at SHAEF. No one there believed that the Germans had the material capacity to launch a concerted counter-offensive in the west, despite growing evidence to the contrary. By the beginning of December ULTRA had inadvertently been rendered ineffectual by a perplexing German radio silence. The consensus of opinion among the ranks was there was 'something going down' but nobody knew precisely what. This lack of accurate and verifiable intelligence regarding the accumulation of German forces in the west was becoming a problem. Although Bletchley Park had intercepted communications that indicated that some German divisions were being moved west from the Russian front, no one at SHAEF regarded this information as anything more than an indication that the Germans were preparing to defend their country against the Allied offensive scheduled for February 1945.

General Alan Jones, commanding the US 106th Infantry Division, expressed his consternation regarding the disposition of his inexperienced troops who were out on the Schnee Eifel area in Nordrhein Westfalen, which was home to numerous farms and hamlets, connected by barely traversable roads and dirt tracks that followed ridgelines or river valleys. The Eifel plateau has three distinct ridges or ranges; the central is called the Schnee (snow) Eifel. This is where the 106th Infantry Division was located. It's a remarkably picturesque place and the soldiers aptly referred to the villages there as 'sugar bowls'. Despite the aesthetic value of the region, Jones complained that his troops were occupying a potentially dangerous salient that jutted out deep into Germany along the 1st Army front. He had voiced his reservations at a VIII Corps staff

Major General Kenneth Strong, the Assistant Chief of Staff for Intelligence (G-2) at General Eisenhower's Allied Force Headquarters.

meeting. Hodges, Bradley and Eisenhower remained obdurate regarding the defence of the Schnee Eifel and the Losheim Gap.

It wasn't that Eisenhower was unaware of the dangers. He later wrote, 'The risk of a large German penetration in that area was mine alone.' General Jones had argued vociferously that too many of his units were situated in exposed areas out in the valleys where they were potentially very vulnerable. Sergeant John P. Kline, M Company, 423rd Infantry Regiment, 106th US Infantry Division, wrote: 'Our company commander set up his headquarters in one of the enormous Siegfried Line bunkers. The bunker was not completely demolished, as they usually were. The underground rooms were intact and accessible. He had taken a room several flights down. The command bunker was on a crest of a hill. The firing apertures faced west towards Belgium, the backside towards the present German lines. There were steep slopes on either side, with signs and white caution tape warning of "Mine Fields". There was a pistol belt and canteen hanging in one of the trees on the slope. Apparently, some GI had wandered into the minefield. As we entered Sankt Vith, Belgium, older, established troops gave us the normal "new kid on the block" salutations. They yelled at us, "You'll be sorry" and other similar phrases, some not so nice. We set up bivouac in woods on the edge of town. The large pines, looking like huge Christmas trees made the woods quiet, warm and very beautiful. The silence and peaceful surroundings of the pines and snow was a pleasant experience. Particularly after the week near Rouen, France, with rain beating on the pup tents and the hustle and noise of the motor march to Sankt Vith.'

Allied confidence that a successful conclusion to the war remained within reach was bolstered by their command of the skies over Western Europe. The British and Americans had the capacity to mount daily bomber attacks that often comprised over 5,000 aeroplanes, but the German will to resist and the means of resistance, so far as then could be ascertained, remained quite sufficient for a continuation of the war.

According to some estimates, in late 1944 the Third Reich could still call on close to 10 million men in uniform, including 7.5 million already serving in its army. On the strength of this, Hitler believed heart and soul that if Germany could hold on to the Ruhr he still had the capacity to force a stalemate and bring the Allies to the negotiating table. He wrote: 'In the whole of world history there has never been a coalition which consisted of such heterogeneous elements with such diametrically opposed objectives. Ultra-capitalist states on the one hand, ultra-Marxist states on the other. On the one side a dying empire, that of Great Britain, and on the other a "colony", the United States, anxious to take over the inheritance. The Soviet Union is anxious to lay hands on the Balkans, the Dardanelles, Persia and the Persian Gulf. Britain is anxious to keep her ill-gotten gains and to make herself strong in the Mediterranean. These states are already at loggerheads, and their antagonisms are growing visibly from hour to hour. If Germany can deal out a few heavy blows, this artificially united front will collapse.'

Despite Allied intelligence officers having received various warnings that a German attack was looming, none of these reports were specific. There was no mention of numbers, commanders or dispositions of German units. Even when the 28th Division inadvertently captured two German prisoners down on the Luxembourg–Germany border no one believed their claims that a massive German counter-offensive was imminent.

CHAPTER THREE

Tanks, tech and terrain

DESPITE GERMANY'S DWINDLING RESOURCES IN the autumn of 1944, due to the implementation of strict central management, weapons production appeared to improve. But did it? Hitler appointed his close friend Albert Speer as Minister for Armaments, and later promoted him to Minister for War. Between early 1942 and July 1944, Speer's armament department claimed to have more than tripled its output. Speer thoroughly enjoyed publicity and had the capacity to exaggerate his own achievements. Later, he would assert that he wasn't a Nazi, but he had joined the Party in 1931 and from 1933 he skilfully crafted its public image. He imposed his architectural and design abilities on the infamous Nuremberg rallies, the great RNS (Reichnährstand – the German authority over agricultural production and distribution), harvest festivals and the 1936 Olympic Games. He was asked in 1979 by a BBC journalist, 'If you had your life over again which would you prefer? Would you prefer to be a non-entity with a clear conscience? Or somebody who is famous or notorious?' Speer said, 'I prefer to be famous.'

He was after all a ruthless career politician who perpetually benefited

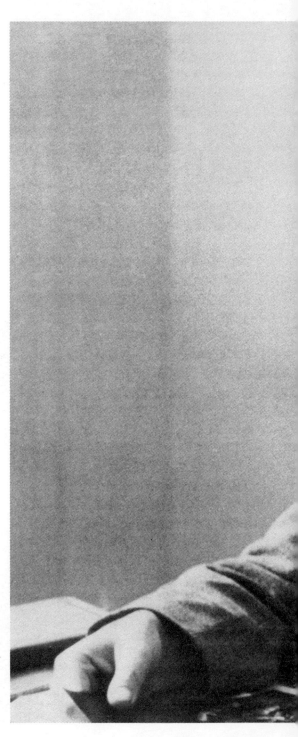

Albert Speer was Adolf Hitler's chief architect and he became the Reich Minister of Armaments and War Production for Nazi Germany during World War II.

from his close personal relationship with Hitler. The increases in armaments production under Speer's auspices were far from miraculous. They were the result of reorganization and rationalization efforts that were initiated long before Speer came to power. He maintained his ideological vision of the war economy as a limitless flow of output released by energetic leadership and technological genius, but the insistence on quantity and the use of forced labour affected the quality of the weapons being manufactured. This didn't prevent Speer from claiming that he was the man who managed to transform the Nazis' weapons production industry. Allied bombing did take its toll but it is estimated that in 1944 the German weapons industry still managed to produce just over a million tonnes (1.25 million tons) of ammunition, 750,000 rifles, 100,000 machine guns, and 9,000 artillery pieces. As impressive as this was, however, it was still only a fraction of the Allied capacity for military production.

One serious deficit was the capacity to produce tanks, but the industry compensated by increasing production of self-propelled assault guns such as the Stug III, Jagdtiger and Jagdpanzer models. With Nazi Germany capable of maintaining production at these levels regardless of adversity, it was still a potentially dangerous adversary. Precisely how dangerous they could be would soon be revealed.

German weapons manufacturers and designers continued to innovate despite military setbacks. One of the recent German inventions had been seen in the field by the US 2nd Armored Division. They reported that they were highly impressed with Germany's new 'Royal' or 'King' Tiger II tank, which packed a devastating high-velocity 88 mm (3.5 in) cannon on its turret that could easily penetrate 5 in (12.7 cm) of armour at a range of up to 2 km (1.5 miles). Moreover, the shells used smokeless powder that made them hard to detect. A tank driver from the 2nd Armored said, 'We had no chance against that monster. I managed to get to a wood, but that sonofabitch kept firing at us. It was terrifying. I didn't think we'd get out of there alive.'

The Germans maintained a qualitative advantage over the Allies when it came to armour. The German King Tiger, Panther and Mk IV tanks were equipped with weaponry that gave them a distinct advantage over the Sherman. Although the Sherman could hold its own against the Mk IV, it was often outgunned by a Tiger or Panther in open ground. The 88 mm (3.5 in) and 75 mm (3 in) guns mounted on the Tiger and Panther respectively were capable of penetrating a Sherman's armour at a distance of up to 2 km (1.5 miles), while the Sherman's short 75 mm gun was incapable of piercing the armour of either German tank at more than 500 metres (0.3 miles), and then it took a lucky shot to penetrate the thick frontal armour of the Panzers. The Americans had begun to introduce upgraded versions of the Sherman with thicker armour and the 76 mm (3 in) gun and, although this improved matters, the Germans still had the advantage, and many American tanks were still of the pre-1942 variety.

When America joined World War II its war economy was initially a little slow on the uptake, but between 1942 and 1944 an astonishing quantity of weapons were manufactured in the USA. This included 50 million rifles, automatic weapons and machine guns, more than two million guns and mortars, more than 200,000 tanks, over 400,000 combat aircraft and nearly 9,000 major naval vessels. Experts claimed that the combat ratio of Sherman tanks was seven losses to one Tiger tank. The thing was, the Allies could replace all seven Shermans but the Germans couldn't always replace the Tigers.

The M4 Sherman was constructed in greater numbers than any other tank during World War II. Praised by some crews and maligned for some for its faults, it became the most iconic tank of World War II. This basic, ingenuous vehicle was perfectly suited for mass production. Between 1939 and 1945 American manufacturers managed to turn out over 55,000 vehicles, well over twice the number of tanks built by Germany during the same time frame. The three elements that distinguished this tank were its reliability, ease of handling and uncomplicated maintenance requirements. On the down side, Allied Shermans had only 5 cm (2 in) of frontal armour, which made the five-man crew vulnerable to various German projectiles. The crew consisted of a driver, assistant driver/bow gunner, ammunition loader, gunner and tank commander. The M4 Sherman was the principal tank in the US Army and Marine Corps armoury during World War II, and remained in active military service from 1942 until 1955.

Early M4 variants mounted a 75 mm (3 in) medium velocity general-purpose gun. Despite its shortcomings, Allied troops still praised the reliable Shermans, but confessed that their American tanks were outgunned and outclassed by the King Tiger II that had a road speed of about 30 km/h (18 mph) on a flat surface. Ernie Jelinek was with the 5th Armored Division, 10th Tank Battalion. Their M4 Sherman tanks were lightly armoured and no match for heavy German tanks and 88 mm (3.5 in) guns. He said, 'My battalion entered the battle with 54 tanks but, in 5½ days, we were down to just five tanks.' He ended up sleeping rough with his crew after various encounters with German Tiger and Panther tanks. 'We were sleeping in foxholes and anything we could find. The weather was cold and we were sleeping in sleeping bags. Then, I was 24 and an army captain when I was involved in the liberation of Luxembourg from the Germans.'

The turrets used on the Tiger II were designed and built by the German industrial giant Krupp, but would inexplicably be referred to respectively as the 'Porsche' and 'Henschel' turrets. It's true that Ferdinand Porsche developed several versions of the tank, each powered by a different engine. The purpose was to build a vehicle with the highest automotive performance possible. However, his designs proved unreliable and none was ever manufactured. The design proposed by rival firm Henschel was approved for production as the Tiger II. The only problem was that Krupp had already been awarded the contract to design and build turrets using the original Porsche design; the problem was there were no Porsche hulls to fit them to, so they were delivered to the Henschel factory. These became the Tiger IIs that took to the field with the curved front turret.

The King Tiger II weighed in at a whopping 68.5 tonnes (75 tons); it featured sloping armour that had a thickness of 15 cm (6 in) on the front hull, which could easily deflect American 75 mm (3 in) and 76 mm (3 in) shells at ordinary distances. It featured an automated turret, which could turn a full 360 degrees in 19 seconds, which was impressive, but theoretically allowed a fast-moving Sherman or an M10 Tank Destroyer to outmanoeuvre the German tanks. Despite its size, the Tiger II was a viable design that possessed surprisingly excellent tactical mobility in open ground. The emphasis being 'on open ground', because on narrow cobbled streets in towns and villages this magnificent beast, with its 89 cm-wide (35 in) treads would become an unwieldy encumbrance. German troops on the move discovered that it was best to dig in and camouflage the tank around towns, whereupon they would wait until the advancing Allies were within 500 yards' range before opening up. The results were often devastating.

German technical innovation extended to aviation, but as impressive as their new jet fighters were, it was all going to be too little too late.

As early as July 1944, Allied pilots had reported seeing German jets in the skies above Normandy. With the Messerschmitt-built Me 262 the German aircraft industry had created an aircraft which could in theory have restored command of the skies over Germany to the Luftwaffe. Compared with Allied fighters of the day it was much faster and packed a much heavier punch.

On 28 August, the first Me 262 was destroyed by Allied pilots when Major Joseph Myers and 2nd Lieutenant Manford Croy of the 78th Fighter Group shot one down while flying P-47 Thunderbolts. The new German jets were impressive but not indestructible. When the Allied pilots became aware that a jet was tailing them, like the Mosquito they would turn as hard as they could just before the jet came into range. The Me 262 could not turn as fast or as tight, so the German would have to go in a big circle and get behind the Allied plane again, whereupon the Allied fighter would repeat the manoeuvre.

As the day of the counter-offensive approached, three German armies comprising more than 200,000 German troops and around 1,400 armoured fighting vehicles were assembled in the Schnee Eifel region of Nordrhein-Westfalen. The terrain there is strikingly similar to that of the Ardennes and geographically it can be seen as an extension of the region. Hans Herbst of the 116th *Windhund* (Greyhound) division was looking forward to tasting American food and smoking quality American cigarettes. He would have one of the luckiest escapes of any soldier in the Ardennes. As Hans Baumann of the 12th SS Division *Hitlerjugend* (Hitler Youth) climbed into the cabin of his Jagdpanzer IV he was in a buoyant mood when he remarked to another member of his crew, 'The weather, particularly the low cloud and mist is on our side. Those Amis have got no chance.' Morale among the German troops was high. Their commanders had promised that these lazy, spoilt American soldiers would be no match for the efficient, disciplined Aryan warriors of the Third Reich.

It's irrefutable that the Nazis had both the methods and the technical acumen, but they didn't have the means of mass production by that stage of the war. German research into the development of nuclear weapons was competitive with American research. German physicists may have made important ground-breaking discoveries in nuclear reactor construction, isotope separation and heavy water production, but their exclusionist, racist policies and twisted ideologies proved ultimately detrimental to scientific advancement. There were a variety of factors

This tank was informally referred to by the German name for the Bengal tiger, 'Königstiger'. This was often translated somewhat erroneously as 'Royal Tiger', and ubiquitously referred to by Allied soldiers as the 'King Tiger'.

that prevented Nazi Germany from achieving the breakthroughs they required to actually construct a nuclear bomb, including governmental interference, and the expulsion, imprisonment and even murder of gifted Jewish physicists and scientists.

The best history provokes cognitive dissonance and it is easy to marvel and even admire German innovation, but what remains is the indisputable fact that under the Nazis there was but one goal: the destruction and devastation of fellow humans. They didn't need to invent WMDs (weapons of mass destruction), they had them already, as they efficiently demonstrated with the death camps and their insane capacity to destroy families, whole communities and exterminate millions of innocent, promising lives.

For all the technical innovation, the German army was restricted by its incapacity to operate at anything below regimental level without orders. They didn't really possess the capacity to improvise as well as the Allies could, particularly the US troops, who could operate autonomously down to squad level when the situation demanded. The Allies' ability to work with the terrain and use the topographical features to their advantage when required was going to prove a significant advantage during the coming battle. The Germans may have had better tanks, such as the King Tiger II, but they needed terrain that was conducive to manoeuvring these behemoths. The Ardennes wasn't suitable, even though German armies had used the area before on no less than three previous occasions. In fact, both sides, despite the weaponry, tanks and military vehicles available to them – and in some case *because* of the weaponry, tanks and military vehicles available to them – had to find ways to deal with the very particular and challenging landscape where they would join battle. It's a topography worth looking at in some detail.

Situated in the southeast of Belgium, the Ardennes is the home of forests of broadleaf trees and fir that extend along hills and valleys bisected by fast-flowing rivers and streams. The Romans called the area *Arduenna Silva* and Julius Caesar was one of the first writers to describe the Ardennes, in his book *The Gallic Wars*, as 'a frightful place, full of terrors'.

It's an area that covers more than 11,000sq km (4250sq miles). The shape of the Ardennes region resembles an isosceles triangle, with a base of approximately 100km (62 miles) at the frontiers where Belgium and Luxembourg meet Germany. The quaint storybook villages of the

Ardennes were replete with winding cobblestone streets and alleys, and gabled and tile-roofed buildings with ornate shutters. Rippling brooks and serpentine streams run through the rolling hills and fields in the green countryside. Castles, monasteries and ruins from the era of Charlemagne can still be found there.

The Belgian Ardennes covers an area that reaches both Luxembourg and northern France in the south and southeast, and Germany in the north. On its western border is the Meuse (also known as Maas) River, and just over the German border to the east is the Schnee Eifel, just below the Hürtgen Forest. In the south, the Belgian Ardennes join the French Ardennes and the Semois River, to the east it has the Our and Sauer Rivers, both running through Luxembourg. The Meuse is a major river, which flows some 925km (575 miles) from its origins in France, north through Belgium and then through the Netherlands where it empties into the North Sea.

There are three specific areas in the region. The northern sector that was zeroed as the trajectory for Dietrich's 6th Panzer Army has the 'High Fens' and the Amblève Valley that extends all the way from Amel (Amblève) to Aywaille and has many impassable steep hills that are definitely not conducive to large tank and troop formations. There are five Belgian towns in the Amblève Valley along the course of the Amblève River and are in relatively close proximity to each other. From east to west they are Amel, Stavelot (not far from Malmedy), Trois-Ponts, Remouchamp and Aywaille. One of the tributaries of the Amblève River known as the Lienne Creek runs south-by-southwest from Targnon to Habiemont. All would become crucial during the Battle of the Bulge.

The area that has the city of Verviers, and the Condroz River in the northwest, sits on an elevation known as the Herve Plateau and consists of low, rolling hills and reasonably navigable areas. There is some open terrain south of Stavelot, between the towns of La Roche and Vielsalm and, down in the southwest corner, there's the sizeable forest of St Hubert. The 165-km long (102 mile) Ourthe River that twists and winds along the towns of Houffalize, La Roche-en-Ardenne, Hotton, Durbuy, Hamoir and Esneux is a tributary of the Meuse River. The Ourthe is formed at the confluence of the Ourthe Occidentale (Western Ourthe) and the Ourthe Orientale (Eastern Ourthe), west of Houffalize.

Manteuffel would attack into the central sector, which has the city of Bastogne. This is the main city in the Belgian province of Luxembourg

The workhorse of the Allied armies, the Sherman M4 was the most widely used tank in World War II. It was reliable, cost effective and available in significant numbers.

that rests on an elevated plateau and has a commanding view of the surrounding area on a clear day. Being centrally located, it became a key strategic objective for both sides during the battle. Another important city there is Sankt Vith in the German-speaking area, nestling behind a high-forested ridge to the east known as the Prümerberg. The nationality of the residents there changed four times in the last century.

The average altitude in the Ardennes region is roughly 488 m (1,600 ft). And there are definitely no mountains. Running through the central section of the Ardennes is another distinguishable terrain feature known as the Famenne Depression, which is a long, narrow valley that extends from the upper Ourthe River near the Belgium–Luxembourg border westward through Houffalize–Marche–Rochefort to the Meuse River near Dinant and Civet. The terrain there is relatively open countryside, with a few mainly planted forests.

General Erich Brandenberger's 7th Panzer Army would attack Luxembourg. Prior to the outbreak of World War II the Belgian and Luxembourg governments invested heavily in the road networks that would make the Ardennes and the Duchy of Luxembourg more attractive to tourists. All the main roads were surfaced with tarmacadam, and ten all-weather roads traversed the German frontier into Belgium and Luxembourg between Monschau (in Germany) and Wasserbillig (in Luxembourg). There were still a lot of minor roads and dirt tracks that appeared on Allied maps as real roads. At the time of the Battle of the Bulge there wasn't a single main road that went in a straight east–west direction through this area. Brandenberger would find horse transport very useful there. There are some boreal-forested areas along with planted forests, but also a number of precipitous valleys and hills. Along the border with Germany in the north of Luxembourg there's a high ridge that was known as 'Skyline Drive' to the GIs, but in the northern sector at Elsenborn there's a similar feature that had the same name attributed to it.

The different terrain in the three main sectors would ultimately demand different tactics. Then there would be winter weather conditions to contend with. The weather had already afflicted many Allied troops, but some of the German units that were assembling east of the Ardennes had been in Russia and had the clothing to deal with sub-zero temperatures. In December 1944, the German infantry used a battle drill and tactics that were dependent upon rigid pre-apportioned guidelines and strict orders. The American emphasis was more orientated to the individual soldier and small-unit tactics. The impending battle would highlight the value of small units, along with designated or assumed effective leadership, and the capacity to be able to act autonomously. This would be a determining factor as the situation evolved.

CHAPTER FOUR

The Allied situation

IN EARLY DECEMBER THE ALLIES were far too preoccupied with preparations for an attack toward the Rhine River to contemplate any other potential scenarios. Monty's 21st Army Group anticipated crossing the Rhine north of the Ruhr while Patton and his 3rd were poised to launch an offensive toward the Rhine from the south. The only static area was the thinly-held Ardennes sector, but plans were afoot to commit these troops to attacks elsewhere. The general consensus of opinion among the Allies inclined strongly toward launching a fresh offensive, when the weather permitted.

The primary goals for the Allies in early December 1944 were focused on preparations for an all-out offensive that would bypass the Ardennes to the north and commence in early 1945. Eisenhower wanted to maintain the momentum by keeping pressure on the Germans. He emphasized that the main thrust toward the Rhine would occur in the north, but that there was also sufficient Allied military resources available near the Moselle south of the Ardennes to go forward to the Rhine, bearing in mind that the north would have priority. On the basis of this he gave permission for Patton's 3rd Army, supported by the 7th Army, to make preparations for an offensive in the Saar region scheduled to commence on 19 December. At the same time, Eisenhower added a cautionary note for his friend General Bradley, saying that he would allow that offensive one week to achieve favourable results.

Albert Honowitz, B Battery, 796th Anti-aircraft Artillery Automatic Weapons Battalion, 3rd Army, wrote: 'We were given a large tent for our crew of seven men. We picked up a stove in the neighbouring small town just across the way and picked up some straw to sleep on. During the day we'd have two men on the track, which were the alert guard in case of an enemy plane attack on the artillery. No planes were ever encountered. At night we'd pull one-man guard in the warm tent, leaving part of the tent flap open so that we could look out.

'Good chow would be brought to us by Jeep. At that time we were receiving our Christmas packages and mail from the States began arriving in as little as six days. In between chow time we'd be having more chow. The in between chow was the packages from home, chicken which we'd swipe from the town across the way, and potatoes, which we'd always swipe. Fried potatoes were our speciality and what we ate the most of. Our bellies were always so full of potatoes that many times we couldn't wait for Army chow.

'The weather was cold, rainy and sometimes it'd snow. When the weather warmed up a little, rain would fall and make the ground muddy – in some places a foot deep. On cold days it would snow. We were very thankful to have this large tent, which could easily accommodate three or four more fellas than the seven that were in it. Our AA [anti-aircraft] set-up was considered a good deal here. This was our first good deal here. This was our first good AA set up since we began operations with the 10th Armored Division.'

While detailing their plans, SHAEF clarified their intention to provide sufficient materials and men for the main effort in the north, and that any crossing of the Rhine from the south was to be restricted until the success of operations in the north was assured. On the basis of this the British and US commanders worked in concert to improve their positions north of the Ardennes. General William Hood Simpson's 9th Army eradicated pockets of German resistance near Juelich, east of the Hürtgen Forest, and by mid-December his forces had reached the Roer River, but he was reluctant to orchestrate an actual crossing while the Germans held the dams on the Urft and the Roer Rivers to the south. On his right flank General Courtney Hodges' forces had advanced under great duress through the Hürtgen Forest and also reached the Roer. At this juncture General Bradley directed Hodges' 1st Army to launch an attack to seize this objective that would commence on 13 December and be halted by other events just three short days later.

Between 10–15 December John Schaffner, Scout, Battery B, 589th Field Artillery Battalion, 106th Infantry Division, said: 'The 422nd Infantry Regiment, which the 589th Field Artillery Battalion was supporting, was occupying the first belt of pillboxes of the Siegfried Line, which had been cracked at this point the previous fall. The Germans were well dug-in opposite the 422nd in pillboxes and held other defensive positions in the area of the Schnee Eifel, a wooded ridge about three miles to the front. The enemy communications center for this area was Prüm, which was at maximum range (12,000 yards) for A Battery. During this period there was little activity other than a few patrol actions. Few observed missions were fired due to the poor visibility. The battalion did, however, have a substantial unobserved, harassing program that was fired every night. The forward observer adjusted by sound, using high-angle fire, which made it necessary to re-dig the gun pits. Alternate positions were selected and surveyed by the survey officer and his party. There were some reports of enemy activity but nothing, apparently, more than routine truck and troop movements. Headquarters Battery crews reported being fired upon on the 15th and that night an enemy recon plane circled the area for an hour or more. Numerous flares were seen to the flanks of the battalion and an enemy patrol was reported to be in the area. During this period most of my time was spent at various outposts near the battery position. There was nothing to report. At night, watching across the snow-covered fields, one's eyes tended to play tricks. On more than one occasion an outpost guard would fire away at some movement out in front of him, only to find out in the morning that he had "killed" a tree stump or boulder.'

Meanwhile, on 15 December 1944, four US divisions held a 143 km (89 mile) front that ran from just below Aachen in Germany, through the Ardennes region to Luxembourg. The 28th US Infantry Division had been dispatched south to occupy part of this innocuous, quiet sector where they could rest and re-equip. Their number had been reduced by four-fifths during the terrible battle in the Hürtgen Forest, where whole companies were reduced to just a few men in some of the bitterest

American infantrymen are served chow en route to La Roche, Belgium in January 1945.

fighting endured by any soldiers in World War II. They badly needed some R&R.

The same applied to the 4th US Infantry Division, who needed to replenish their seriously depleted ranks down in the Duchy of Luxembourg. One GI of the 4th needed to attend to some pressing, or rather itching, personal hygiene issues. John E. Kunkel, Company L, 3rd Battalion, 22nd Infantry Regiment, said, 'I would like to relate something that took place a day or two after we were relieved in the Hürtgen and pulled back to what I recall was an old German training camp. A short time after we got there, we were all given a bunk and a grey German army blanket. Well, about midnight it happened, we all started to itch all over. My buddy said he felt something crawling on his neck. I took my pen flashlight out and, sure enough, there they were, body lice. Now the problem was getting rid of the lice. About daylight we found an old kerosene lantern. We poured the kerosene into a steel helmet and, with an old dirty sock, we all took a sponge bath. It was hard on the skin, but we got rid of the lice. It was some time until we could take a real bath with good old water. We started to smell to the point we all smelled like Billy goats, it got to where we could not live with one another.'

While recuperating, the battered US divisions down in Luxembourg were treated to USO (United Service Organization) shows presented by big Hollywood stars of the day such as Bing Crosby, who expertly provided mental sedation by crooning to the GIs in his inimitable fashion. He was great but he had some staunch competition from German-born, husky voiced Hollywood star Marlene Dietrich, who wowed the GIs wherever she appeared. She had sizzled on-screen with the best leading men but Ms Dietrich's most memorable co-star was General George S. Patton. While entertaining the troops during World War II, she ventured within a mile of the German front lines on the arm of the general, who personally gave her a brace of Colt 45s to see off potential assassins. The Nazi government had placed a seven-figure bounty on the Berlin-born actor's head. She had become a US citizen in 1939, flatly refusing a personal request from Adolf Hitler to return to Germany as the centre-piece of his propaganda campaign. Marlene Dietrich actively supported the Allied cause throughout the war.

One of the US divisions that had been sent to the Ardennes and surrounding area had never fired a shot in anger. On 12 December, the 106th Infantry Division occupied positions previously held by the 2nd

John Schaffner, Scout, Battery B, 589th Field Artillery Battalion, 106th Infantry Division. He is wearing his 'Golden Lion' arm badge of the 106th.

GIs from E Company, 110th Regiment, 28th US Infantry Division, in the Hürtgen Forest near the Raffelsbrand road junction.

Infantry Division, who assured the nervous young GIs that 'this was the quiet sector and they would be able to catch up on some rest there'. The mission of the 106th was to defend a 40 km (25 mile) wide salient that extended beyond the Siegfried Line into Germany. Their three infantry regiments, the 422nd, 423rd, and 424th occupied a line from north to south along the Siegfried Line. The supply depot in closest proximity was located over 55 km (34 miles) west at the small town of Noville. The northernmost 8 km (5 miles) of the 106th flank was defended by the 14th Cavalry Group, which bordered on the boundaries of the relatively inexperienced 99th Infantry Division, who were defending an area known as the Losheim Gap on their north.

The Losheim Gap referred to the 9.5 km (6 mile) wide hole in the Allied line that existed between the 106th and the 99th Infantry divisions. By the end of November, General Courtney Hodges' 1st Army was covering an area that extended almost 150 km (93 miles) from the German town of Aachen in the north to the border of Luxembourg and France in the south. On his left, Major General 'Lightning' Joe Collins' VII Corps held 25 km (15.5 miles) of the line from Aachen to the Hürtgen Forest in the Hohes Venn (high fens) region. In his centre was Major General Gerow's V Corps, holding the next 25 km (15.5 miles) that stretched all the way to Losheim. On his right was Middleton's VIII Corps that held almost 100 km (62 miles) of front from Losheim to the boundary with General Patton's 3rd Army in the south.

Hodges wasn't completely impervious to the risk he was taking by expanding the line beyond the capacity of the units in the field. He had voiced his reservations to both General Omar Bradley and General Eisenhower. Bradley furrowed his brow while Hodges spoke and inter-rupted him to say, 'First, when anyone attacks, he does it for one of two reasons. Either he's out to destroy the hostile forces or he's going after a terrain objective. If it's terrain he's after then he feels he must either have it himself or deny it to the other fellow.' Hodges pointed to the topographic map laid out on the table before the generals and indicated the terrain features before saying, 'If they come through here we can fall back and fight a delaying action to the Meuse. Certainly, we can slow them down until you hit them on the flanks.' This appeared to pacify all present and the meeting drew to an amicable close.

The 106th were covering a front that extended deep into German territory and covered almost 30 km (18.5 miles), when military guidelines had stipulated that an effective division front should not exceed 9 km (5.5 miles). To the north of them the 99th Infantry Division fared no better. The 99th was also stretched beyond what they could reasonably be expected to hold in the event of a German offensive.

On 15 December, the 99th began attacking some German pillboxes. Seymour Reitman, 2nd Battalion, 395th Regiment, 99th Division, remembers that they captured five of these and took 13 Germans during the fighting. It was at this point that Seymour got an ominous request from one of the sergeants, who said to him with a knowing wink, 'Take these prisoners back to battalion, and I don't care if they get back there.' Seymour immediately understood what the sergeant was implying and retorted, 'Screw you, that's not me.'

In the autumn of 1944 Eisenhower's forces were comprised of three army groups. The 21st under British Field Marshal Bernard Law Montgomery in the Netherlands to the north, the 12th under General Omar Bradley in Belgium and Luxembourg in the centre, and the 6th under General Jacob Devers in southern France and the German Saar region. Eisenhower was responsible for all operations in Western Europe, including supporting naval and air components. The chain of command at the front line meant that Major General Troy Middleton, Commander, VIII Corps, reported to Lieutenant General Courtney Hodges, Commander, 1st Army. His immediate superior was General Omar Bradley, who kept his good friend General Eisenhower, Commander, Supreme Headquarters Allied Expeditionary Force (SHAEF) reliably informed of all developments. It did not end there, because Monty reported to Field Marshal Alan Francis Brooke, 1st Viscount Alanbrooke, Chief of the Imperial General Staff (CIGS), and the professional head of the British army, during World War II. Ike reported to General George Marshall back in Washington DC, who was ultimately responsible for the war both in Europe and the Pacific.

The chain of command meant little to the men who were going to do the actual fighting as opposed to those moving pieces around on a map well behind the lines and out of harm's reach. In total there were almost two million Allied soldiers in the Western European theatre, but only four unsuspecting US divisions stretched out between Aachen in Germany and Luxembourg held the Ardennes region. They had no preconception of the gargantuan struggle they were about to endure.

Down in the Alsace region of France, General Patton was uneasy

General Omar Nelson Bradley, nicknamed Brad, was a senior officer of the United States army during World War II. He was also a personal friend of Eisenhower and had studied with him at West Point.

about the large gap that existed between the 1st and 3rd Armies, and he was not renowned for reserving his opinions. He observed: 'There are still six million Krauts who can pick up a rifle,' and went on to say, 'The 1st Army is making a terrible mistake in leaving VIII Corps static, as it is highly probable that the Germans are building up to the east of them.' Patton, who often professed his knowledge of military history, had placed his 3rd Army in the Alsace region of France. He was convinced that the Germans were still capable of mounting a major counter-attack but erroneously assumed that it would occur there. He wasn't getting it all his own way at that time, however. In the 12th Army Group's southern sector, Metz had proved to be a particularly difficult objective, and fighting there had continued almost unabated since 8 November.

One of the critical problems facing Eisenhower on the eve of the Battle of the Bulge was a severe shortage of infantrymen. General Omar Bradley had reported on 15 December that, owing to casualties incurred by inclement weather-related conditions and the previous combat, his army group had a deficit of around 17,000 riflemen. In response to this Eisenhower ordered the reclassification of as many support personnel as possible so that they could be re-designated as infantrymen. Up until this time, most African-American soldiers in the European theatre had been assigned to service units. Now these troops were permitted to volunteer for duty as combat infantrymen, with the understanding that after the necessary training they would be committed to front-line service. At that time race was still a deeply divisive and contentious issue in the US military. Eventually, some 2,200 African-Americans were organized into 53 platoons and assigned to all-white rifle companies in the two US army groups. The exigencies of combat had temporarily forced the US army to discard its policy of segregating white and black soldiers.

On 25 June 1941, President Roosevelt had signed Executive Order 8802. The act banned discrimination in the government and defence industries stating that, 'it is the policy of the United States to encourage full participation in the national defense program by all citizens of the United States, regardless of race, creed, colour, or national origin, in the firm belief that the democratic way of life within the Nation can be defended successfully only with the help and support of all groups within its borders.'

In October 1944 Patton delivered a characteristic speech to the men of the all-black 761st tank battalion. 'Men, you're the first Negro tankers to ever fight in the American Army. I would never have asked for you if you weren't good. I have nothing but the best in my Army. I don't care what colour you are as long as you go up there and kill those Kraut sons of bitches. Everyone has their eyes on you and is expecting great things from you. Most of all, your race is looking forward to you. Don't let them down and, damn you, don't let me down!'

The 761st would perform brilliantly and, according to one soldier, they never conceded an inch of ground. Two other black units, the 969th and the 333rd Field Artillery Battalions, were also present during 1944–45. However, despite orders from President Harry Truman in 1948 to integrate black soldiers into the US military, separate units were maintained during the Korean War, which lasted until 1953.

On 7 December 1944, Allied commanders including Eisenhower, Montgomery and Bradley attended a meeting in Maastricht. The main topic on the agenda was about renewing the attack beyond the Roer to the Rhine. It was agreed the 2nd British Army would strike south-east-ward from Nijmegen between the Maas and the Rhine Rivers while the US 1st and 9th navigated the Roer and headed east. This move would entail at least one of these armies turning north to link up with the British. It was assumed that by the time this attack went in, the 3rd Army presumably would also be in proximity to the Rhine. As soon as this was confirmed Eisenhower would launch two thrusts across the river in force, with the 21st Army Group and the 9th Army north of the Ruhr in conjunction with the US 1st and 3rd Armies south of the Ruhr.

Bradley tentatively agreed to this modus operandi, but said that the main priority for the Allies was to capture the Roer dams before launching an all-out offensive. His other concern was the recent inclement weather conditions that prompted his suggestion to postpone all offensive operations until 15 January 1945 at the earliest. No mention was made during this meeting of the alleged massing of German forces east of the Ardennes.

By 15 December everything was quiet in the Ardennes town of Bastogne. The locals had really taken to these fresh-faced young Americans and many lifelong friendships had been established. One resident of Bastogne said, 'We shared everything with the Americans, but some of the things they gave us in return were really not edible, and a Hershey bar was definitely not real chocolate.'

Major General Troy Middleton had established the VIII Corps head-quarters in Bastogne at a former Belgian army base known as the Heintz Barracks, which had been used by the Germans as a recruiting station, among other things, during the occupation. Middleton had fought in World War I, had an excellent combat record and was regarded by both Bradley and Patton as one of the best tacticians in the US Army. His tactical acumen would soon come in very handy. American lieutenant Ernest Gessener, of the 28th US Infantry Division, was officially the first American killed in Bastogne when it was liberated on 11 September 1944, but he wouldn't be the last by a long chalk. In early December some GIs of the 28th were still in and around Bastogne.

John Schaffner, Scout, Battery B, 589th Field Artillery Battalion, 106th Division, wasn't happy about the location of his unit. He said, 'In a position like this, every member of the gun crew had to stand guard duty at night. This included me and the sergeant. I will tell you, that first night was very nerve-racking. Not knowing very much about the situation or from what direction the enemy might come, every sound was a cause for concern. Two hours felt like eight. The severe cold made it even more difficult.'

Out on the Schnee Eifel, Jim Cooley and another GI of the 106th US Infantry Division stamped their feet to stave off the gnawing cold that permeated every sinew. He spoke in hushed tones about Oklahoma and complained about having to pull guard duty at that godforsaken hour. In the distance they could hear the faint rumble of engines but couldn't determine if they were German or Allied vehicles. Jim peered, snake-eyed, into the murky dense fog, shrugged his shoulders and blew into his cupped hands before saying, 'Sounds like somebody is on the move buddy.' The other GI inclined his head: 'Is it ours or theirs?' Jim smiled. 'Hard to say.' Then, suddenly, a yellow flash illuminated the pre-dawn gloom. A split second later a thunderous, guttural boom, followed by what sounded like a banshee scream, pierced the mist. Jim dived on to the frozen earth and pulled his helmet down. More 'screaming meemies' exploded in close proximity. The other GI took a direct hit and burst into bloody pieces that impacted the ground like meat on a butcher's slab. It was 05:30, 16 December 1944.

CHAPTER FIVE

The German situation

KNIGHT'S CROSS RECIPIENT ERWIN KRESSMAN, *Hauptmann, 1 Schwere Panzer-Jäger-Abteilung 519* (Commander, 1st company, Heavy Tank hunter Battalion), attached to the 6th Panzer Army, had been fighting the 'Amis' (Americans) in the Hürtgen Forest. Charged with the arrogance of youth and Nazi indoctrination, he didn't regard them as a particularly dangerous enemy. Erwin hadn't slept much that night. He always had that same feeling of excitement and trepidation before an offensive. It was hard to sleep with so much adrenaline pumping through his veins. During the previous evening he had complained of having a headache and one of his crew had given him a small white tablet. He'd noticed the name Pervitin printed on the small tube. It was widely available among the German soldiers during World War II. 'Will this cure my headache?' Erwin asked. 'I don't know but I haven't got anything else so you will have to make do like the rest of us,' replied the crew member. These days it's better known as crystal meth, and could keep the troops awake for days.

Immediately after morning roll call, Erwin gathered his crew and stepped outside to inhale a deep breath of freezing air. Then he walked

Knight's Cross recipient Erwin Kressman, Hauptmann 1 Schwere Panzer-Jäger-Abteilung 519 (Commander, 1st company, Heavy Tank hunter Battalion), attached to the 6th Panzer Army.

over to his 41 tonne (45 ton) Jagdpanzer and patted the 100 mm (4 in) thick sloping metal hull before getting inside and giving orders to start up the engine. He beamed to himself as the Maybach engine chortled and spluttered into life. Then he opened the hatch and stood upright in the cupola with the upper half of his torso protruding out of the machine. 'Vorwarts', he shouted at the top of his voice that was quickly drowned by the sound of throaty engines starting up. Erwin waved his right arm in the 'advance' gesture. He couldn't feel any pain. It was game on and he felt that this was going to be a big one.

While Hitler was recuperating from the failed attempt on his life in July 1944 he began ruminating on the prospect of mounting a major offensive in the west. Granted, Field Marshal Montgomery didn't initially consider the capture of Antwerp and its port a priority, but Hitler was well aware of its strategic importance. He thought that it was time for the German army to seize the initiative and take the fight to the Allies, and he'd been pondering various scenarios. It's fair to say that the one-armed, one-eyed Colonel Count Claus Schenk von Stauffenberg probably provided some of the impetus behind Hitler's plans to mount a counter-offensive in the west. His relations with his generals had been deteriorating for years, but after Stauffenberg's failed attempt on his life at the *Wolfsschanze* (Wolf's Lair) near Rastenberg on 20 July 1944, they were understandably at an all-time low.

High-ranking German generals noticed that the Fuhrer's demeanour had changed quite radically. He appeared nervous and visibly drained. He spoke in short staccato sentences and rarely looked his subordinates in the eye when he addressed them. Any officer who dared to disagree with him could quickly find themselves the unwitting recipient of a foam-mouthed, apoplectic rant. General Heinz Guderian noted that: 'Hitler believed no one anymore. It had been difficult enough dealing with him. It now became a torture that grew steadily worse from month to month. He frequently lost all self-control and his language grew increasingly violent.'

There may have been an obvious explanation for his erratic behaviour. In late autumn 1944 Hitler was dealing with some serious health problems. His health had gradually deteriorated after the July assassination attempt. His doctor, the half-Jewish Theodor Morell, kept a medical diary of the drugs, tonics, vitamins and other substances he administered to Hitler, usually by injection (up to 20 times per day) or in pill form.

Hitler had a weak stomach, so he preferred injections to pills that he often had trouble digesting. The problem was that Morell's experiments sometimes contained toxic and addictive compounds, such as heroin. It has even been suggested in some quarters that Morell's drug combinations were instrumental in accelerating Hitler's already deteriorating health. In November 1944 some of those close to Hitler became so concerned that they even attempted to remove the doctor, whom the Fuhrer trusted so implicitly.

There's every indication that Hitler was addicted to an opiate drug known as Eukodal that was frequently administered by Morell. Witnesses said that the effect of the drugs on the Fuhrer was nothing short of miraculous. One minute the Fuhrer was so frail he could barely stand, the next he would fly into an apoplectic rage and rant at whoever was unfortunate enough to be in close proximity. This erratic and unpredictable behaviour is highly characteristic of addicts, and Hitler was no exception. The Nazi architect Albert Speer had become a close confidante of Hitler and noticed the drastic changes in his demeanour. 'He would drum his fingers impatiently and speak in quite short, staccato sentences. His eyes had a haunted look, typical of someone who was heavily addicted to drugs,' said Speer in an interview after the war. 'When I saw him in the autumn of 1944 he was no longer the dynamic, mesmeric leader that I had known in the past.' Albert Speer surpassed Herman Goering in Hitler's inner circle popularity stakes that almost every top Nazi aspired to.

During the months that followed the assassination attempt, Hitler invited his generals to propose several plans for a major western offensive. He may have earmarked the Ardennes for the location of his counter-offensive based on the historical precedent. The German army had successfully used this route before on no fewer than three previous occasions – in 1870, at the beginning of the Franco-Prussian War, in 1914 as part of the von Schlieffen plan, and again in 1940. Nevertheless, it's safe to say that these considerations were not paramount in Hitler's mind at that particular time.

For the second time in a century, Germany would be fighting and maintaining a war on two fronts. The strategic and operational problem posed by this was almost as old as Germany itself and had often been analysed, with solutions previously proposed by the great German military thinkers Helmuth von Moltke, Alfred von Schlieffen (who masterminded the invasion of Belgium in 1914), and Erich Ludendorff. Travelling by the theoretical route, they had arrived at the conclusion that Germany lacked the strength to conduct successful offensive operations simultaneously in the east and west.

The OKW (*Oberkommando der Wehrmacht*, or German Armed Forces High Command), with its chiefs Wilhelm Keitel and Alfred Jodl, saw the Western Front as the paramount theatre of operations. The Reich's famous tank commander, Heinz Guderian, the man who could choreograph tank movements with the precision of a ballet, sincerely believed that the fate of the war would be settled in the east. Guderian didn't unduly surmise this opinion, because statistically the German forces lost eight out of every nine soldiers fighting the Russians.

Meanwhile, Hitler was so confident that his plan would succeed that he even guaranteed inclement weather, which became known as 'Hitler weather', to his men on the ground. His meteorologist Werner Schwerdtfeger accurately predicted that during the first seven days of the German counter-offensive, dense mist and fog would critically limit the use of Allied air power. In retrospect this prediction was a pretty safe bet. Rivers and streams bisect most of the valleys and plateaus in the Ardennes region. Combined with the surrounding planted and boreal forests, this naturally produces misty conditions during the late autumn and early winter.

Hitler may have discussed the operational concept of a counter-offensive through the Ardennes with General Alfred Jodl before the 16 September edict. Evidence suggests that Jodl and a few of his subordinates from OKW had studied the Ardennes concept intensely and based their views on various factors. Ground for manoeuvre in the Ardennes area was limited and would therefore require the use of relatively few divisions. The terrain to the east of the breakthrough sector selected was densely forested and would provide excellent cover from Allied air observation and attack in the days preceding the assault. If German forces could slice through the divisions in this region they could, in principle, eliminate the Allied advance to the Ruhr. These were all the reasons Hitler needed.

Other major reasons for Hitler's selection of the Ardennes were based on the following premises. Firstly, Alsace-Lorraine was out of the question because Patton and the whole 3rd Army were there, and secondly, according to the Abwehr, or German intelligence, the Ardennes sector

Field Marshal Walther Model, one of the few German officers who dared to disagree with Adolf Hitler in 1944. He gave the German plan a ten per cent chance of success.

was very thinly manned. Hitler assumed that striking a decisive blow here would force a breach between the British and the Americans and lead to political as well as military disharmony between the Allies. Furthermore, an entrance along this breach would isolate the British 21st Army Group and allow for the encirclement and destruction of the British and Canadians before US forces could react. The third factor was based on logistical reasons. The distance from the jump-off line to the strategic objective (Antwerp) was not too great and could be covered quickly, even in bad weather. The only serious natural obstacle to the German advance was the Meuse River that runs from north to south through the Ardennes region.

While the OKW agreed to the plan in theory there were other sugges-tions on the table. Field Marshal Walther Model, commanding *Heeresgruppe 'B'* (Army Group B), proposed a classic pincer offensive codenamed *Herbstnebel* (Autumn mist), designed specifically to ensnare and destroy Patton's 3rd Army and Lieutenant General William H. Simpson's 9th Army between Luxembourg and eastern central France in the region to the north of Colmar. Hitler would eventually use this name, although the plan that transpired was quite removed from Model's original conception. The other plan designed by von Rundstedt's staff, simply called 'Martin', was based on the tried and tested Nazi Blitzkrieg formula and intended to drive through the thinly-defended Ardennes, dividing the Allied armies in two and culminating in the recapture of Antwerp and its valuable port.

Relations between Hitler and Gerd von Rundstedt were not particu-larly good and hadn't been for some time. The general had a lofty, arrogant disposition that didn't endear him to his colleagues. During the Allied invasion of Normandy, Rundstedt was severely restricted regarding the deployment of German troops. This was primarily due to the fact that Hitler maintained his opinion that the D-Day landings were merely a diversionary tactic to detract attention from what he thought would be the real landing site at Calais. This also prevented Rundstedt from deploying armoured reserves. The situation resulted with Rundstedt being sacked by Hitler on 1 July 1944 and replaced with General Günther von Kluge, although Rundstedt received the Knight's Cross as compen-sation for his efforts. It wasn't the first time that Hitler had sacked him and it wouldn't be the last. On 1 September 1944, Rundstedt was appointed commander-in-chief of the entire Western Front

(*Oberbefehlshaber West*) and was recalled by Hitler. The resounding defeat of the British Airborne at Operation Market Garden was inaccurately credited to Rundstedt rather than Model, who was the real orchestrator of their demise.

In October 1944 Rundstedt stuck his neck out when he informed Hitler through General Field Marshal Wilhelm Keitel that it would be 'better to end the war with a negotiated peace settlement'. Hitler sacked him again, but quickly revoked this impetuous decision because the truth was that Rundstedt was one of the very few German officers he trusted. After being re-appointed as commander of the western forces, Rundstedt collaborated in the planning of the *Herbstnebel* operation. The title may have sounded innocuous but it had a sinister and ominous Wagnerian connotation. In his operas Wagner used the presence of mist and fog to announce the seasonal return of darkness, and to introduce audiences to the Norse interpretation of fog as a means to permeate light and goodness.

The only problem with both plans for an offensive in the west was the inability of the Luftwaffe to provide adequate air support because the Allies had largely decimated their numbers. It's a well-recorded fact that during one meeting Hitler asked Herman Goering precisely how many aircraft he could get into the air to support this offensive. 'Three thousand, *mein* Fuhrer,' replied Goering, to which Hitler retorted with a somewhat uncharacteristically sardonic smile, 'I think that two thousand will be enough.' Is it remotely possible that both of them knew that neither of these numbers was feasible at that time?

Hitler finally opted for Rundstedt's plan and decided to transpose it to his own designs. On 16 September Hitler made the first announcement of the prospective counter-offensive in the Ardennes during the meeting held at OKW headquarters. He subsequently imposed this plan on the German high command, and compelled everyone involved to the strictest secrecy. Only the actual planning staff would be informed of developments, and even though it was overtly apparent that hundreds of officers would have to be involved in the actual handling of troops and supplies during the concentration period, the number of those in the know would be drastically limited. This entailed a major reshuffle of headquarters that started around 10 November 1944.

Field Marshal Walther Model was in fact one of the very few high-ranking officers who openly dared to disagree with Hitler, despite the latter's insistence that this plan would inevitably succeed and divide the Allies piecemeal. The superbly self-confident and frequently abrasive Model finally acquiesced to the Fuhrer's plan and orchestrated the real tactical groundwork during the planning stages. Model had had a tremendous reputation as a Panzer commander and had also been responsible for defeating the Allies that had opposed his forces during Operation Market Garden. Model believed the scheme for an offensive in the west was beyond the capacity of the available resources, and consequently he preferred the option of a smaller offensive. These protests didn't resonate with Hitler, who was resolute that the plan could succeed.

Model later remonstrated that one concerted thrust above Aachen with all available German forces would be more effective than this three-pronged attack. Hitler continued to disagree vehemently, basing his opinions on the assumption that there was already a glaring lack of cohesion among the generals at Allied command. A crushing defeat against them would restore crumbling German morale and be the proverbial final straw. There had indeed been some disparity at SHAEF regarding the advance toward Germany after the Normandy campaign, but this didn't effectively detract from the fact that the Allies were still materially in a considerably stronger position than their German adversaries. The residual capacity of the Allies, particularly the Americans, to produce weapons and armaments far exceeded those of German industry in 1944.

Model continued to protest to other senior commanders that Germany's limited resources would ultimately prevent their armies from achieving their objectives. He was quoted as saying, 'This plan hasn't got a damned leg to stand on.' Just before the attack took place he changed his stance slightly and gave it a 'ten per cent chance of success'.

Nevertheless, Hitler fervently believed that the time was right to launch a concerted strike against the Allies. It would go ahead.

Three very different generals commanded the three German armies earmarked for the main offensive. The 6th SS Panzer Army that was selected to be the spearhead was commanded by Josef (Sepp) Dietrich. Born in Hawangen, near Memmingen in Bavaria, on 28 May 1892, he was the illegitimate son of butcher Kreszentia Dietrich. In 1911 he volunteered to join the Bavarian army and in World War I he received the Iron Cross, first class, while serving with the 4th Bavarian Field Artillery Regiment. He had been a dedicated Nazi since 1928, when he

Field Marshal Karl Rudolf Gerd von Rundstedt during World War II. He joined the army in 1892 and was one of the oldest serving commanders in the Third Reich.

Josef 'Sepp' Dietrich, the butcher's son from Bavaria, commanded the 6th Panzer Army in the Battle of the Bulge. He held the highest commissioned rank in the SS.

became a member of the *Schutzstaffel* (SS) and was personally selected by Adolf Hitler to become one of his bodyguards. Dietrich actively participated in executions of political opponents in the 1934 purge known as the Night of the Long Knives. Due to his close relationship with Hitler he was promoted to *Oberstgruppenführer und Panzer Generaloberst der Waffen-SS* (SS four star general), a position that far exceeded his military acumen. One of his contemporaries described Dietrich as a mentally unstable, violent fanatic and alcoholic. In late 1944, Hitler appointed him commander of the 6th SS Panzer Army. His sycophantic behaviour may have endeared him to the Fuhrer but there were those who seriously doubted Dietrich's military and strategic acumen. General Wilhelm 'Willi' Bittrich, who had commanded the 2nd Panzer Corps during Operation Market Garden once remarked, 'I once spent an hour and a half trying to explain a situation to Sepp Dietrich with the aid of a map. It was quite useless. He understood nothing at all.'

Despite his critics, Dietrich warranted his reputation for displaying courage. His subordinates generally regarded him as a tenacious and ambitious commander, but by December 1944 he had become a volatile alcoholic and his drinking was becoming a problem. One German general said, 'That butcher's son from Bavaria can neither see nor think straight anymore let alone command a whole army.' His designated task was to provide the spearhead with his 6th Panzer Army, which would extend from Monschau in Germany to Krewinkel just over the border in Belgium. The initial terrain wasn't particularly conducive to extensive tank and troop manoeuvres because the attack front was considerably narrower than those allocated to the two armies to the south of his position. If Dietrich could successfully navigate the first piece of terrain he would reach the high fens (*Hohes Venn* in German; *Haute Fagnes* in French) that would then provide relatively open country with few geographic obstacles to prevent his progress. It didn't occur to anyone at the time to provide a workable 'plan B', just in case his forward units were forced to make a detour.

In December 1944 the son of German Foreign Minister Joachim von Ribbentrop, Rudolf von Ribbentrop, was serving with the 12th SS-Panzer division, *Hitlerjugend*, where he had been wounded in Normandy. He said, 'The Americans were preparing for an offensive from Aachen to the Rhine and were pounding us hard with their artillery. Every artillery barrage that preceded this one paled into comparative insignificance.

The plan for the offensive in the west was an irresponsible gamble and Germany would suffer as a result.'

'I hadn't planned on joining the SS at all, in fact. I wanted to be a policeman,' said Hans Baumann, also of 12th SS *Hitlerjugend*. 'While I was at the recruiting office in Aachen, before the city was destroyed, I was approached by a representative of the SS who told me that "real men" joined the SS, not the paltry police force. He made a very convincing case that was good enough for me. I joined the SS and that was that.'

Manfred Toon Thorn, who was with the 1st SS-Panzer Division, *Leibstandarte SS Adolf Hitler*, said, 'We participated in the Ardennes Offensive. When people read about the experiences of a tank regiment they rarely imagine themselves inside a tank actually driving it. They either do not know or cannot imagine how the war looks through a 25 cm-square window. That is how it is for a "tankie" when he drives to the front, however, and that's how it was on 16 December 1944. In the very early hours of the morning, in accordance with our orders, we left the cover of the Schmidtheimer forest and struck out west.'

While Dietrich commanded the main thrust in the north, in the centre Panzer Troop General Baron Hasso-Eccard von Manteuffel, a member of the Junker aristocracy, had been appointed as commander of the under-provisioned 5th Army. He had served under Erwin Rommel, and, having studied under innovative tank genius Heinz Guderian, he was regarded as an armoured specialist. In September 1944, Manteuffel was summoned to Adolf Hitler's military headquarters at Rastenburg, where he was given command of the depleted 5th Panzer Army and assigned to Army Group G on the Western Front. After enduring heavy combat in the Alsace against Patton's 3rd Army, the 5th Panzer Army was taken out of the line and transferred to Army Group B in the Eifel region of Germany, where they began refitting in preparation for the coming counter-offensive. Manteuffel was a studious and intelligent commander who disagreed with the original operations plan. He managed to persuade Army Group B commander Jodl that certain tactical amendments needed to be made if the proposed plan was to have any chance of success.

Manteuffel was a good general but he didn't particularly want to cross swords with Hitler because he was aware of how volatile he was at this time. First, he approached Model to explain his reservations and secure the field marshal's support. During the final planning conference at Hitler's HQ, Manteuffel and Model effectively joined forces and managed to achieve certain modifications to the original plan. Hitler agreed to commence the artillery barrage at 05:30 instead of 08:00. Manteuffel wanted to capture the first major Belgian town in the path of the 5th Panzer Army, despite the general aphorism that all defended towns should be circumnavigated. Sankt Vith still had working rail links to Germany and could be used to block potential Allied reinforcements. By the end of the conference Manteuffel was relatively optimistic about the plan but he still had reservations. He wasn't comfortable about having Dietrich and the 6th Panzer Army on his northern flank, but there could have been other reasons apart from tactical ones for this. Manteuffel wasn't overly enthusiastic about having so many SS units on his right flank.

Placing a German army comprised of regular soldiers alongside an army that was made up of mainly SS units had on occasion proved problematic in the past. The relationship was a complex one. The SS units were usually given priority regarding equipment and materials and had a tendency to demean Wehrmacht units. The propensity of certain SS units for committing atrocities among civilians and enemy combatants was also a source of disdain to many Wehrmacht officers. Despite this, there remained a moral heterogeneity among the German forces and the Wehrmacht maintained a grudging respect for the combat prowess of the Waffen-SS, even if they did display a tendency to divert from the plan and behave like pirates. This occasionally made it difficult to co-ordinate military operations.

One particular unit in Dietrich's 6th Panzer Army had gained a gruesome reputation on the Eastern Front. *Kampfgruppe Peiper* (Peiper Combat Unit) was known as the 'Blowtorch Battalion' due to their insane capacity to burn and murder every potential obstacle in their path. Himmler's 'Golden Boy', Joachim 'Jochen' Peiper, commanded them. He had served as first military adjutant to SS leader Heinrich Himmler, and even married one of Himmler's personal secretaries, Sigurd Hinrichsen. Although Peiper had been a fanatical adherent to the National Socialist cause he wasn't a member of the Nazi Party. At the time of the counter-offensive he was 29 years old, one of the youngest regimental commanders in the German army, and someone who advocated and possessed the kind of fanaticism Hitler admired. Peiper had been purposefully chosen to lead the spearhead because he was an exponent of tough SS leadership, regarded as being charismatic and extremely loyal to his unit who wholeheartedly trusted him in return, even under the most extreme conditions. Within the Waffen-SS the 1st Division was considered one of the most efficient. But there was a dark side to Peiper. He had the capacity to be completely ruthless. After Germany invaded Poland in September 1939, Peiper accompanied Himmler almost everywhere he went on official SS business. This allowed Peiper to be present at the execution of 20 Polish citizens just weeks later in Bydgoszcz Blomberg, an event that was part of Hitler's special assignment for Himmler to 'eliminate intellectuals'.

In the ensuing months, under Himmler's auspices, Peiper took on even more, assisting in the creation and implementation of policies intended to control the Polish populace. Peiper was present at the gassing of Polish psychiatric facilities; was alongside SS troops at the Battle of France; and attended meetings of Reich leaders, during which Peiper was privy to Hitler's plans for war. In January 1943, Peiper was promoted to *Sturmbannführer* with the 1st SS Division and fought at the Battle of Kharkov, where he was awarded the Knight's Cross and German Cross in gold. He fought with 1st SS in Russia until July 1943. Then, after refitting in Italy, the division was sent back to the Eastern Front where Peiper was awarded the Oak leaves to his Knight's Cross, earned by his leadership in action near Zhitomir. The *Leibstandarte* incurred heavy casualties during the winter fighting in Russia, and in April 1944 they were transferred to Belgium to rebuild. By this time Peiper had been promoted to *Obersturmbannführer* and given command of Panzer Regiment 1.

Even though Peiper was a combat veteran, he still hadn't grasped the logistics of organizing an invasion column, and from the outset he would create gridlocks that would seriously impede his progress. Moreover, he was showing signs of battle fatigue.

Commanding the German 7th Panzer Army in the south along the Luxembourg border was General Erich Brandenberger. Despite having an impressive combat record, Brandenberger had been given the task of pushing through to the Meuse River and placing a secure cordon of infantry and artillery facing south and south-west. Once this had been established his 7th Army would anchor the southern German flank on the angle formed by the Semois and Meuse Rivers. Hitler was specific that this cordon should extend as far west as Luxembourg City. The purpose of this manoeuvre was firstly to encircle the town of Echternach,

General Hasso von Manteuffel commanded the 5th Panzer Army.

Joachim Peiper, also known as Jochen Peiper, was a field officer in the Waffen-SS. In the early years of World War II he served as personal adjutant to Heinrich Himmler. During the Battle of the Bulge he lead Combat Unit (Kampfgruppe) Peiper.

and secondly move through the Duchy of Luxembourg in order to block Patton's advance if he decided to move his 3rd Army northwards.

Brandenberger was a studious and methodical commander who had seen a lot of action on the Eastern Front, and although he wasn't particularly well liked among his peers and often derided for being a typical product of the general staff system, he was nonetheless a competent leader. It wasn't his intention to orchestrate a breakthrough to the west on the southern shoulder of the attack front. Brandenberger had considerably more modest ambitions that entailed preventing counter-attacks from General Patton's 3rd US Army, rather than launching a major drive to the west in tandem with Manteuffel in the centre and Dietrich in the north. Brandenberger had been present with other commanders and their chiefs of staff at the initial briefing by Rundstedt.

During the night of 15 December, front-line units of the 106th noticed and heard what they considered to be increased activity in the German-occupied sectors out on the Schnee Eifel. The 28th, further south in Luxembourg, also reported an increase in enemy activity along the east bank of the Saar River. The information was duly relayed to Allied headquarters that remained dismissive. Three German armies had managed to surreptitiously manoeuvre themselves into position almost under the noses of the Allies. The battle was about to begin.

CHAPTER SIX

What the hell is going on?

IT WAS 05:30 ON THE morning of 16 December 1944 when the eerie silence that pervaded those gentle rolling hills out on the frozen Schnee Eifel was shattered. 'The vortex of a tornado is a vacuum,' said John Hillard Dunn, Company H, 423rd Regiment, 106th Division, 'and that is where we were, in the centre of a storm of armour and artillery storming forward into the Ardennes.' Along the whole Allied line from just below Aachen to Luxembourg, Nazi *Nebelwerfers*, five-barrelled mortars (nicknamed 'Screaming Meemies'), artillery pieces and tanks unleashed their hellish fury on unsuspecting US troops. That first day was one of incredible flux and chaos as the rage of Nazi Germany was released against many untried and untested American troops.

Phil Burge, Co. C, 55th Armored Engineer Battalion, didn't have a clue what was going on when the German offensive began. 'We were in Metz resting and recuperating after the Battle of Metz, where one of my good friends stepped on a landmine. We had no idea. Maxwell Taylor was back in Washington, nothing was going to happen, this offensive

German troops advance past burning American vehicles, 16 December 1944.

just got everybody by surprise. It was just unthinkable that it was happening. We left Metz in the rain.'

Some German troops penetrated deep into the Allied line while others remained static waiting for roads to clear. Some GIs panicked while others dug in deeper and held on with all the courage and fortitude they could muster. It was a day that remained with most of the incumbents for the rest of their natural lives. Some of those who survived would attempt to dispel those first torturous hours from their memories, but no one who was there and lived to tell the tale would forget that first day. They would see comrades blown to smithereens and run the whole gamut of emotions from abject terror to almost divine relief. On the Allied side the attack was received with shock and disbelief: 'Why didn't we see this one coming?' 'What the hell is going on?' and variations on that theme were among the reactions from the GIs in the foxholes and the generals in the SHAEF HQ boardrooms.

When the initial devastating barrage hit on that freezing cold morning in December, the pastoral calm of the Schnee Eifel was immediately transformed into a raging inferno of apocalyptic proportions. In the distance, unsuspecting GIs could see innumerable pointillisms of light dissecting the murky surroundings as 2,000 guns, ranging from 3 in (7.5 cm) mortars to giant 16 in (40 cm) railway guns, erupted simultaneously and began impacting along the entire American front line. Soon after the initial German barrage had dissipated, three German armies began to seep out along a 143 km (89 mile) front. Shocked sentries of the 106th 'Golden Lion' Division out in Germany were still reeling when they heard footsteps crunching through the snow as German infantrymen began menacingly emerging from the dense mist like feral spectres.

The 99th Division's 394th's Intelligence and Reconnaissance platoon was led by 20-year-old 1st Lieutenant Lyle J. Bouck, Jr. Bouck's platoon had conducted frequent patrols into Germany to scout the terrain and observe enemy movements. Sometimes they returned with German prisoners for interrogation. But they never encountered evidence of the impending German attack on 16 December. During a transfer of divisions in the area around Elsenborn Ridge, Bouck's platoon was ordered to defend the position near the German-speaking Belgian town of Lanzerath. Holding and defending a position was not the designated task of an intelligence and reconnaissance platoon, but it was a case of all hands on deck at that moment, and Bouck had no doubt his men could do the job. On the morning of 16 December, Bouck was surprised by the sound of shelling. The area in front of his platoon was hit, and the shelling was moving closer and closer to his position. Luckily, the firing overshot their position. Bouck wanted to mount an ambush on Germans in Lanzerath, but his position was revealed. Digging in on a hill, Bouck's men repelled three German frontal assaults, but during a fourth assault the Germans flanked Bouck's position. Surrounded and out of ammunition, the men of the I&R platoon gave up the fight and reluctantly surrendered. Their efforts had engaged a significantly larger German force for an entire day, allowing other American units time to regroup and prepare defences. For their efforts, all 18 men in the platoon received the Combat Infantryman's Badge and the platoon was awarded the Presidential Unit Citation. Bouck received the Distinguished Service Cross.

Joseph Littell, Company I, 422nd Infantry, was attending to his morning ablutions in the latrine when the storm broke. With his pants still around his ankles, squatting over the slit trench in that frigid morning air, he was one of the first to see hundreds of tiny flashes on the horizon. His personal business was rudely interrupted by the ominous whoosh of incoming artillery landing in close proximity. The GI attempted to remedy his predicament and draw up his pants before stumbling and falling face first on the snow-covered ground. As murderous fragments zipped overhead in all directions, the GI squeezed a copy of *Stars and Stripes* with one hand and cupped his genitals with the other. The publication had been intended for both reading matter and cleaning his backside. Lying there with his trousers around his knees and his bottom still dangerously exposed, here was at least one GI who was 'going commando' that morning. 'I was covered in shit, mud and shrapnel and I wasn't planning on making any sudden moves,' he said. 'But after the bombing I think it would have taken more than one edition of *Stars and Stripes* to clean my ass, and I would have needed both hands.'

John Schaffner was deep in his dugout when it started. He'd weighed up the odds and decided that being in a dugout was probably better than being back with the rest of Battery B. He said, 'Early in the morning, before dawn, at 06:05, on 16 December our position came under a barrage of German artillery fire. I was on guard at one of our outposts. I got down in the lowest possible place and attempted to crawl into my helmet. I was trying to get down as far as possible but I found my buttons to be in the way. During the shelling, many rounds exploded real close and

Twenty-year-old 1st Lieutenant Lyle J. Bouck wearing the checkerboard arm badge of the 99th Infantry Division 'Battle Babies'.

showered dirt and tree limbs about, but also there were quite a few duds that only smacked into the ground. Those were the "good" ones as far as I was concerned.'

Initial American casualties were light but in some places the shelling severed telephone lines to the rear, impeding communications between the troops. German infantry advanced in semi-darkness through the pre-dawn mist, their path illuminated in many places by carbon arc lamps that created a kind of artificial moonlight bouncing off low-hanging clouds. As their infantry moved doggedly forward, German Panzer columns waited irascibly in the rear for them to clear the roads ahead so they could begin their frantic bid to reach Antwerp.

Over at 1st Army HQ the news that something was afoot down in the Ardennes was greeted with incredulity. But as the day wore on it was evident that these were most definitely not simple probing attacks. As German 88s and *Nebelwerfers* wrought havoc among front-line US divisions, the magnitude of this onslaught was becoming glaringly apparent. The 1st Army decided to release Combat Command B, 9th Armored, to VIII Corps at 10:25, allowing General Middleton to displace his Combat Command R, 9th Armored, to provide support for the 28th Infantry Division. 'Well, we repelled the first group that came up. And, I don't know, we fought them for maybe 15 minutes or 20 minutes. It wasn't a very long fight. But because they were coming up a very steep hill, up to where we were at the top of the hill, we were in a perfect position. And then after about another half hour or so we were pretty quiet,' recalled Pfc (Private First Class) Ralph Frank Youngmann, 9th Armored Division. 'We didn't hear much. We could hear them whistling and bugles blowing and horns going off. And lights were shining through the fog. You could see the lights from the other side of the river. Finally, they started to hit us from the right I think this time, trying to get up. There was a draw running down along our right flank. And we were spread out so thin we couldn't even see the outfit on our right or the outfit on our left. And a couple of our guys got hit. One squad was completely surrounded and they were captured. The first, I think, the first or second charge that came up, they were taken. It was our machine gun squad. So they were our first real casualties of the Battle of the Bulge that I knew of. We had a couple of other firefights, which weren't very organized. They were just a few riflemen shooting at us from different angles and so forth. But it was very frightening, especially for the kids that had never seen this much.'

The 4th Infantry Division situation in Luxembourg on the morning of 16 December when the Germans attacked was far from favourable. At that time every single infantry battalion in the 4th was considerably under-strength. Three battle-weary regimental combat teams were holding a front that ran approximately 56 km (35 miles) and extended along the west banks of the Sauer and Moselle Rivers in Luxembourg. Communications between the battalions there were already strained because of the shortage of radio equipment. At least in the eventuality of casualties there were suitable medical facilities behind the lines with the latest equipment and well-trained staff. They had lost over 5,000 battle casualties to date and a further 2,500 had succumbed to trench foot, exposure and combat fatigue. In addition to this the division had been in continual action since Normandy, and by December 1944 much of its equipment was dilapidated and unreliable.

Dorothy Barre, serial number N-752 051, was an American nurse working with the 16th General Hospital when it was sent to Liege, Belgium. She was on duty at 05:30 on 16 December. She said, 'We were a complete unit with casts, dental equipment, X-ray machines, surgical equipment, everything. I worked in the surgical orthopedic wards. When the Bulge broke, we were in tents that would hold 30 patients at a time. In the center of each tent was a potbelly stove that kept us warm, and we had surgical carts we could use for dressings. Liege was an ammunition dump, so they were sending buzz bombs toward the city. We were in that alley of buzz bombs, and we were hit three times with the buzz bombs, not where the patients were. We did not have any casualties. We were ten or 12 miles from the fighting. But one time one of the buzz bombs hit nearby, one of the houses, and we admitted Belgian patients. I had a mother and a daughter, and the daughter died. The doctor and I worked together to help them until they could get the mother to the Belgian hospital in Liege.

'When the Bulge started, we got wounded from army trucks or stretchers. They might just be wrapped in blankets, the young fellas, and we got them washed up. Sometimes we would have four nurses to one guy, getting them washed up, pyjamas on, their dressings checked. We would ask them if they had pain, and we carried codeine and aspirin in our pockets. I remember sitting on the cots and talking with the guys. They would always ask me where I came from, since I have a Boston accent. Sometimes they would stay with us for just eight or ten hours.

The patients would get a good meal and cleaned up and given penicillin too. After they were well enough, they were flown to Paris or London. We had a few specifically from the 101st paratroopers and engineers as well. I think we knew that the Germans had broken through and the Bulge was getting close to us. We didn't go into the city, about four miles away. We stayed in a chateau, a stone building. I was on the third floor, and there were seven to eight nurses to a room with a potbelly stove in the center. We had showers down in the cellar. Some nights, some of us would go down in the cellar because of those buzz bombs. They would start them about 11 o'clock at night and go until about two or three in the morning, and then they would start again at four in the morning.'

That morning as flares of red, green, amber and white irradiated the pre-dawn sky, the men of the 106th quickly realized just how exposed their position was out on the Schnee Eifel in Germany. Ground-shuddering explosions accompanied the incessant blasts of German artillery. Apart from severed telephone cables, attempts to relay information were further disrupted due to radio frequencies getting jammed by the Germans. Someone at SHAEF had jokingly referred to the 106th sector as 'Honeymoon Place'. Well, the honeymoon was now well and truly over. The combined destinies of the 106th Infantry Division and the 14th Cavalry Group were inextricably linked on that first fateful day. Once the barrage had lifted in the 106th sector, a chaotic tableau confronted forward observers, who reported traffic jams and American convoys heading west with headlights glaring while flares and tracers zoomed overhead. Some reports claimed that the German patrols were breaching the front line.

Further south along the Luxembourg–Germany frontier the 28th Infantry Division was also in the path of Manteuffel's 5th Panzer Army. The two Panzer corps on Manteuffel's left flank shattered the thin lines of the 28th Division and soon reached the outskirts of Houffalize and Bastogne. After only marginally surviving the terrible Battle of the Hürtgen Forest, the 28th was once again thrown headlong into the fray to face overwhelming waves of German troops. During that first day of the assault five German divisions crossed the Our River heading west. The 28th's 110th Regiment was covering over 18 km (11 miles) in the centre of the division sector. It received the full brunt from Manteuffel's men.

Positioned astride one of the major roads leading to Bastogne, the 110th received orders to hold at all costs. Fighting from a series of isolated strongpoints, the 110th absorbed the full fury of the German attack and offered stiff resistance. Benjamin Elisberg was a Pfc with the 3rd Battalion, 110th Infantry Regiment, when the first waves of Germans attacked. 'We had an observation post and I remember seeing a lot of enemy activity, vehicles moving around, and this was reported over the radio that we were observing a lot of German activity. At that time I remember somebody saying, "well don't worry about it, we'll keep it monitored or something and see what happens". And I remember during that time they gave me a three-day pass to go into some town to have fun. And that's where the Germans counter-attacked and I was trapped in a building. I remember this guy saying a tank was coming up the street and I opened up the back door and bullets came flying in as somebody opened up an automatic weapon. I closed the door, then I remember running upstairs looking out a window and a couple a Germans were out there throwing grenades. I tried I guess to get them in the window. I fired my rifle. That's it. Then they stopped moving. And we were running downstairs again and getting a grenade from the lieutenant, throwing the thing out as far as I could and firing stopped. I said, I told them let's get outta here.'

From the very first day the division and regimental headquarters lost all ability to control the battle. Their forces were simply too scattered and the German attack too immense.

Down in Luxembourg the situation was becoming equally dire. At around 06:00 hours on the morning of 16 December reports from Major General Raymond Oscar 'Tubby' Barton's 4th Infantry Division, 12th Infantry sector, where the terrain was exceptionally rugged, disclosed that there had been some light enemy patrol activity but no cause for alarm. When the attack hit, many towns and villages became the unwitting targets of powerful artillery barrages that lasted several hours and were accurately directed at command posts, severely disrupting all wire communications.

Within a short time the enemy began to infiltrate 4th Infantry Division's forward positions with reconnaissance forces that were later reinforced with substantial infantry formations of the full-strength 212th *Volksgrenadier* Division. Reports covering those first few hours were scant because of the lack of wire communications and the initial failure of radios, particularly those at outposts, which had a very limited range over the uneven terrain around Echternach and Berdorf, often referred to as 'Little Switzerland', and it was only by late afternoon that a clearer picture of the situation began to develop. This was an all-out German offensive.

The first objective of Dietrich's 6th Army, Hitler's spearhead, was to overcome any resistance on the Elsenborn Ridge. To assist the attack there the 6th Army committed two *Volksgrenadier* infantry divisions to provide the 'gap' through which the Panzer spearheads would penetrate. The US 99th Division, a green, untried unit that had arrived in theatre in November, was defending the area. Road networks into the twin villages of Rocherath and Krinkelt became critical objectives for the assault. Though surprised, overwhelmed and isolated by the attack, small-unit heroics in the 99th were successful in holding back German attacks. The young men of the 99th, many of whom were attending the same college when they enlisted, earned their title 'Battle Babies' by pitting their wits against the brute force of the Nazis. The obsequious *Obergruppenführer* Sepp Dietrich had neither the talent nor the military knowledge to cope with sizeable Panzer forces, particularly in terrain that wasn't conducive to the movement of large troop and tank formations. He was a poor choice.

The in joke among the 99th at the time was that they were looking forward to 16 December because Marlene Dietrich and her USO show were scheduled to perform for them. Instead of Marlene Dietrich they got Sepp Dietrich and were ostensibly aggrieved by this. It was a poor trade. Despite repeated attacks by German forces, the 99th held out.

Hans Baumann of the 12th SS Panzer Division was in the thick of the fighting on 16 December. He remembered: 'Some of us were stuck on the other side of the Elsenborn Ridge. My company encountered very strong resistance at Krinkelt and Rocherath and suffered many casualties there. I was driving a heavy Jagdpanzer and clearly heard the shells whizzing past. Some exploded close by and shook my vehicle. We were very well trained to deal with these situations and didn't expect such a strong fight from the Amis. Suddenly, I felt a tremendous crash as a shell impacted the flank of my vehicle. I don't know what fired the shell, whether it was artillery, a bazooka or a Sherman. I still don't know.' The claustrophobic compartment in the Jagdpanzer began to fill with black, asphyxiating smoke. Hans realized that his vehicle had been hit. 'I struggled to open the hatch and free myself. Most of my crew and myself managed to jump out and run for cover. Our radioman was stone dead. A sizeable piece of shrapnel was protruding from his abdomen and his intestines were steaming out beneath the wound. That was the closest that I came to being killed in the battle.'

The Allied situation out on the Schnee Eifel was becoming increasingly precarious for the men of the 106th. Manteuffel's 5th Panzer Army had effectively begun surrounding two regiments of this ill-fated division. At 09:45 General Jones sent ominous instructions to his 422nd and 423rd Infantry Regiments: 'Expect to clear out area west of you this afternoon with reinforcements. Withdraw from present positions if they become untenable.' General Middleton called General Jones to inform him that reinforcements were on the way, but they wouldn't get there until 07:00 the following morning. It wasn't going to be easy to move a column of reinforcements along muddy roads, over the rugged and snow-bedecked terrain of the Ardennes at night. The move could be further exacerbated by the confusion that was surfacing as some forces attempted to hold their positions while others were perfectly happy to leave the area.

Dispersed along the Ardennes front when the German attack erupted were three combat commands of the US 9th Armored Division. Combat Command A was just south of the confluence of the Our and Sauer Rivers between the 109th Infantry Regiment of the 28th Infantry Division to its north and the 12th Infantry Regiment of the 4th Infantry Division to its south. Combat Command B was near the village of Faymonville 15 km (9 miles) north of Sankt Vith. Combat Command R was positioned at Trois Vierges, roughly 26 km (16 miles) north-east of Bastogne, Belgium, in support of VIII Corps' left and centre. 'Somebody asked me once,' said a veteran of the 9th, '"Where were you in the Battle of the Bulge sir?" I looked him straight in the eye and answered with one word: everywhere.'

Major General Troy Middleton's US VIII Corps did not expect an attack of this magnitude. He hadn't sufficiently established an organic system of mutually supporting dug-in defensive positions in depth to cover the occupied ground. The current organization as it stood relied too heavily on fragmented points of defence astride rivers such as the Our. His four divisions, the 4th, 28th, 106th, and the 9th Armored, along with the 14th Mechanized Cavalry Group and a reconnaissance regiment, were covering a front that meant they were so thinly dispersed that all

Hans Baumann, Jagdpanzer driver, 12th SS Division 'Hitlerjugend' (Hitler Youth).

these units were vulnerable to enemy attack, and now they were realizing precisely what that entailed and how precarious their situation was. In the centre of this position and down to the south the Germans were slicing through the gaps like a hot knife through butter.

Robert Kennedy was a language specialist who worked as a German translator and later he joined the 65th Infantry Division. At the time of the attack he was with XIX Corps that operated as part of the US 1st and 9th Armies. He recalled, 'I was there the first morning that we got the surprise attack. We got up and were near Aachen, just outside the town in a suburban area. The front was just down a little ways. We heard all this firing and wondered what it was, and it was German firing. They were firing over our heads back at the replacement depots, and they had a lot of heavy artillery. Then we found out that the Germans had passed us over and made a turn and presented a front to the south. We were strung out east and west, and back behind us were the British, who were facing the German front. In fact, before we came out of the sack, we heard the firing, and I recall a lot of firing. It was a miserably cold morning, and the streets were terrible with ice. There was nothing much we could do because we did not know what was going on, and they did not advance toward us, just toward the front lines.'

On 16 December 1944 at the Hôtel Trianon Palace, in Versailles, Eisenhower began the day reading yet another message from Monty. In this one the field marshal was requesting official permission to travel home for Christmas. The message also made reference to a light-hearted wager the two had made on 11 October 1943. Monty predicted that the war would not be over by Christmas 1944. Eisenhower had thought it would. Monty had written, in his own handwriting, 'For payment, I think at Christmas'. Ike replied that he still had nine days to go. The bet was still on.

General Omar Bradley had been hearing fragmentary reports of some enemy activity in the Ardennes, but it didn't deter him from getting in his staff car and heading to Versailles for his planned conference with Eisenhower. When Bradley left Luxembourg City he was oblivious to the fact that just 25 km (15.5 miles) away to the east the Germans were attacking in force. The planned conference was attended by Air Chief Marshal Sir Arthur Tedder, and Generals Walter Bedell Smith, Harold R. Bull (his chief G-3 [part of the American military intelligence operations]) and Kenneth Strong. The subject they wished to address concerned infantry replacements, but during the discussion the proceedings were suddenly interrupted when American deputy G-2 Colonel Thomas J. Betts entered the conference room and delivered a message to Major General Ken Strong.

Strong nodded and furrowed his brow as he received the information. Then he stood up, reminiscent of a best man at a wedding reception, and audibly cleared his throat. In slow measured tones worthy of any 'Keep calm and carry on' British tradition he spoke, 'Gentlemen, your attention please.' All present directed their eyes to him and listened. The meeting was a freeze frame when he read aloud, 'This morning the enemy counter-attacked at five separate points across the 1st Army sector.' The statement was received with hushed exchanges as the officers digested the news. One other version of the events claims that Strong said, 'The enemy have attacked Middleton's VIII Corps boundary.' Bradley's face registered a half smile as he shook his head and insisted that it was just a spoiling attack intended to draw Patton's troops out of the Saar. Eisenhower realized the magnitude and intent of the day's encounters. He interrupted Bradley's diatribe with a stern look on his face. 'This is no spoiling attack, Brad.' The information appeared to sink in. Walter Bedell Smith stood up and walked around the large conference table to Bradley, placed a reassuring hand on his shoulder and reminded the general that he had been hoping for a German counter-attack. Bradley reciprocated that he had indeed, but added, 'I'll be damned if I wanted one this big.'

Eisenhower acted immediately, issuing orders to dispatch the 10th and 7th Armored Divisions to the Ardennes. It was a seminal moment in the story of the Battle of the Bulge that highlighted the opacity of previous intelligence reports, because these divisions would play an integral part in helping to stem the momentum of the German assault. Throughout the meeting Bradley remained in denial concerning the nature of the attack, despite the fact that the 1st Army's G-2 had already received a captured copy of Rundstedt's Order of the Day transmitted to SHAEF plainly illustrating the German objectives.

Despite open resistance from some of his subordinate commanders including Bradley, the following day Eisenhower would commit the strategic reserve 82nd and 101st Airborne Divisions.

By the evening of 16 December, in the 106th Division sector, General Alan Jones had committed all his available reserves and the situation was deteriorating alarmingly. One GI of the 424th Regiment had been anticipating a good breakfast of hotcakes, doughnuts and coffee that morning when a sergeant interrupted the proceedings and shouted with great urgency: 'They've broken through Cannon Company, and Company C is going up to plug the hole.' Suddenly mess kits clattered to the frozen ground as the breakfast line dispersed and the soldiers ran to grab their equipment. Some were lucky enough to grab a doughnut en route. As the men assembled, eyes widened as enemy shells began falling in relatively close proximity. The gnawing feeling of hunger and trepidation induced some to vomit, as this would be their first combat experience. They obediently clambered into their 'deuce and a half' (two-and-a-half ton) trucks and headed out east to meet the enemy as fast as they could go. Private First Class Royce E. Lapp, Weapons Pit, C Company, 424th Regiment said, 'The front line was fluid and we didn't know how far the Krauts had come already. Our trucks were open and we were ready to jump out at any time. It was a mad dash for a couple of miles up the road before we were fired on and piled out. We soon began to see what was waiting for us up ahead. We saw that a fellow can be a beat-up bloody mess and still walk. These boys making their way back to the aid station were not a pretty sight. All we could do was stare at them as they passed and wonder when it would be our turn. The line hadn't given and bent or fallen back; it had been chewed up right where it was with massive artillery fire and overwhelming infantry assault.'

By the close of that first day the Germans had pitted roughly 200,000 men against 83,000 Americans. At their spearheads, the Germans had at least a 6-to-1 advantage in infantry and a 4-to-1 advantage in superior armour. All along the Allied line the tide of resistance ebbed and flowed as German attacks were repulsed in some places, while Allied defence disintegrated in others. In the north, General Leonard T. Gerow, commanding V Corps, concluded that his 2nd Infantry Division, that had actually initiated an attack that day, were in a vulnerable position. He asked 1st Army commander General Courtney Hodges for permission to pull them back and place them with the 2nd along the Elsenborn ridge, a natural line of defence that ran from north to south just west of the German border. Hodges, obviously ignorant of the developing situation, refused the request point-blank. Hodges wasn't popular among his fellow officers and sacked more of his subordinates than any other general in the ETO. Like Bradley he didn't grasp the developing situation.

Gerow on the other hand recognized the scope of the German attack but Hodges, perhaps the least competent senior American commander in Europe, failed to do so. As the realization of what was really happening began to sink in Hodges panicked and abandoned his HQ in the Belgian town of Spa, fearing that advancing Germans would overrun it.

The day hadn't gone particularly well for the US divisions strung out along the 'Ghost Front', but plans were afoot to remedy the situation. The day hadn't gone exactly according to plan for the Germans either. The roads on the northern shoulder had become seriously congested and objectives had not been achieved. Those first 48 hours were absolutely crucial to the German plan, but to some failure was not an option.

World Series 1934?

THERE WAS ANOTHER OMINOUS FACET to this unexpected German counter-offensive, which would resound among almost every Allied unit on the front line and beyond. Hitler had assigned the task of infiltrating behind the Allied lines to SS *Obersturmbannführer* (lieutenant colonel) Otto Skorzeny. With his square jaw and duelling scar on his left cheek, he was almost a caricature of the archetypal Nazi, but he was the man who could be trusted to get things done. His fellow officers regarded him as a highly talented and creative leader who had quite a reputation as a *bon viveur* and a ladies' man. Hitler trusted Skorzeny implicitly and informed him of the plans for an attack in the west before the other field marshals and army commanders.

The Fuhrer had been so impressed by this SS officer's rescue of Mussolini, and his successful kidnapping of the son of Hungarian leader Admiral Horthy, that he assigned him a further mission. What transpired has been frequently misrepresented and misinterpreted. What is indisputable is the psychological effect of what became known as 'Operation Greif' (*'Greif'* being German for Gryphon, the mythical winged beast).

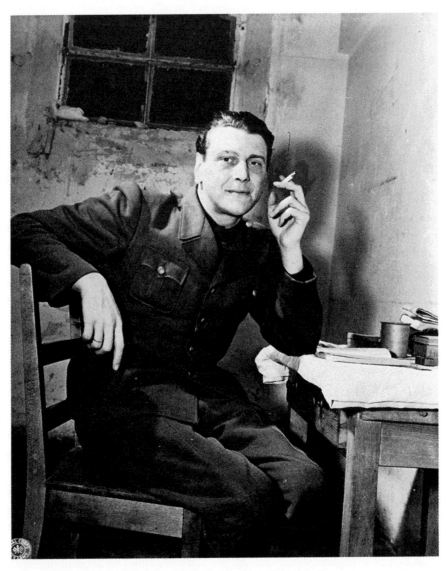

Otto Skorzeny was an Austrian-born SS-Obersturmbannführer in the Waffen-SS. He was aware that under the Hague Convention of 1907, any of his men captured while wearing US uniforms would be executed as spies. He was also known as 'Hitler's assassin'.

The purpose of Operation Greif was to get Skorzeny's commandos behind American lines during the opening hours of the German offensive.

The operation was comprised of two prime components. Ground infiltration, 'Operation Greif', which would be led by Skorzeny himself and an airborne drop behind enemy lines code-named 'Operation Stosser', (*Stosser* is the German word for an ejector pin) under the command of paratroop specialist Col. Friedrich A. Freiherr von der Heydte. This unit was expected to secure vital crossroads along the flank of the German line of advance in the attack zone of the 6th Panzer Army and block the movement of Allied reinforcements. Using captured US army uniforms and vehicles, the specially-assembled 2,000-strong 150th Panzer Brigade, also known as Brandenburger, was given the task of securing several bridges on the Meuse River between the cities of Liege and Namur, in anticipation of the expected breakthrough by the Panzer divisions. The ultimate purpose of German soldiers wearing GI uniforms would be to disseminate dissention and fear among the ranks of the retreating Allied forces.

There were major obstacles from the outset. The 'chosen men' were expected to speak English, or at least have a working knowledge of the English language. In reality, only a handful of these men spoke adequate English and there was a lack of appropriate American uniforms and equipment, which made the deception a precarious venture.

By 1944 Allied intelligence had attributed the title 'most dangerous man in Europe' to Otto Skorzeny, who was also referred to as 'Hitler's assassin'. Despite inadequate planning, Operation Greif was launched in the small hours of 16 December. Skorzeny's men got to work cutting communication wires, issuing fake orders, and turning around road signs. The success of the operation hinged heavily on the progress of Dietrich's 6th Panzer Army on that first day and the assumption that the counter-offensive would be '*fahrplanmäßig*' (on schedule) in accordance with the plan. Skorzeny foresaw the potential dangers and anticipated that if he was successful in seizing the two bridges he'd been told to, it was highly probable that his forces would be isolated by Allied counter-attacks until the main body of the German advance could reach him.

Once the operation got underway word of the German impostors began to get around and the ensuing paranoia amongst American forces even led to some Americans firing on each other. GIs at checkpoints started interrogating any unit or individual they didn't recognize with questions on American popular culture in an attempt to unmask these German agents. Many American soldiers and even Allied generals were detained at checkpoints for wrongly answering questions such as 'Who won the World Series in 1934?' Field Marshal Bernard Montgomery wouldn't have known, and in characteristic fashion refused to show his ID, protesting, 'Don't you know who I am?' The American sentry didn't and shot Monty's car tyres out. Then Monty was unceremoniously hauled into a nearby barn and physically restrained until his identity could be confirmed.

The designated drop zone for Operation Stosser was poorly chosen. It was then and still is a region of steep hills, dense woods and marshy valleys with only one navigable north–south running road that connected the town of Malmedy with the German-speaking Belgian city of Eupen, and still does. It was estimated that was the best avenue of approach along the flank of the 6th Panzer Army. North of Malmedy, a road junction links the town of Verviers with this highway. It should have been glaringly obvious that this terrain was not conducive to the deployment of massed airborne troops.

The physical effect of these operations was limited but the psychological effect was quite profound because within a few short days there were few GIs in the line who hadn't heard of those 'Krauts wearing our uniforms'. The initial effect of Operation Greif affected the Allied traffic, which was occasionally impeded and slowed down by the need to repeatedly stop at checkpoint after checkpoint and provide proof of identity as genuine Americans. When some of Skorzeny's soldiers were captured, they told their interrogators that their mission was to reach Paris and assassinate the Allied supreme commander, General Eisenhower. This was an intentional lie intended to propagate unrest among the higher echelons, which was never actually endorsed by Skorzeny. However, when Eisenhower learned that Skorzeny was leading this clandestine operation the Trianon Hotel in Versailles, which served as his headquarters, was transformed into a veritable fortress. Tanks and machine guns were set up along the perimeter and around the palace, and an Ike lookalike was brought in to lure out any potential Nazi assassins.

One GI wrote of his direct encounter with some of Skorzeny's men, 'The Germans were still attempting to infiltrate our lines dressed like American soldiers and driving 106th Division vehicles. We had just dug in when an American jeep with four men wearing American uniforms came up the road. I got up and yelled, "Halt!" They kept going, but a machine gun on the other side of the road started firing. The jeep stopped, and we went up to them with our guns pointed. The driver and the two in the back showed us their dog tags, but they didn't speak. Next to the driver was a first lieutenant. He showed us identification, but he spoke in King's English. I asked him if he thought Detroit would win the World Series. He said no, but they would put up a bloody good fight. We pulled them out of the jeep because the World Series had been between the Cardinals and the Browns. It was then that I discovered they were Germans in US uniforms. We sent them back to our G-2 intelligence group.'

Although Operation Greif achieved some results, Operation Stosser completely failed to accomplish its mission. Ten aircraft dropped their jumpers near Bonn, over 100 km (62 miles) from the drop zone. Only 35 of the 106 Luftwaffe aircraft involved managed to release their paratroopers over the Hohes Venn area, and only ten planes dropped their loads on or near the planned drop zone. Col. von der Heydte actually managed to reach the intended location but didn't manage to assemble enough men to execute the plan. After missing most of their allocated drop zones the paratroopers became scattered and disorganized. They never managed to assemble a decent fighting force to complete the task of blocking the roads north of Malmedy. The original Stosser plan had been for the battle group to seize and hold the critical Eupen–Malmedy crossroads, and block American attempts at reinforcing or counter-attacking southward along these arteries. Finding themselves outnumbered, freezing and incapable of achieving any of their objectives, the paratroopers of Operation Stosser eventually dissolved into the Ardennes.

On 16 December Skorzeny divided his men into four separate commando teams and dispatched them behind the advancing Armoured 1st Division SS columns in order to flank American forces, some of whom were falling back in their wake. The commandos easily infiltrated the lines and, by the end of the first day, had successfully penetrated 100 km (62 miles) behind the Allied lines and reached an area between the Belgian cities of Liege and Namur that traversed alongside the Meuse River. The problem was the 1st SS Division was not keeping pace. On the following day Skorzeny decided to abort the mission.

Seventeen of Skorzeny's men were captured and executed following trials by military commission. They were found guilty of being in contravention of The Hague Convention concerning land warfare; article 23 states: 'It's especially forbidden to make improper use of a flag of truce, of the national flag or of the military insignia and uniform of the enemy'.

The psychological damage they inflicted far outweighed the material. Serious panic ensued when a German commando team was captured near Aywaille on 17 December, a good 65 km (40 miles) behind the American lines. The team was *Unteroffizier* Manfred Pernass, *Oberfähnrich* Günther Billing, and *Gefreiter* Wilhelm Schmidt. They were forcefully apprehended when they failed to give the correct password at a checkpoint. It was Schmidt who gave credence to the rumour that Skorzeny's unit intended to capture General Eisenhower and his staff.

CHAPTER EIGHT

A day of mixed fortunes

THE WHOLE PREMISE OF THE German plan of attack relied heavily on being able to stringently adhere to the schedule. Selected objectives would have to be achieved on day one and there was little attention given to a 'plan B'. The first difficulties encountered from the outset by *Kampfgruppe Peiper* occurred over at the Losheim Gap, where a serious bottleneck had afflicted the agenda as multiple heavy vehicles attempted to funnel into the small roads. Several crucial hours were lost while Peiper regrouped his spearhead and endeavoured to deal with this annoying disruption to the timetable.

He drove out to the 12th *Volksgrenadier* Division advance command post. This division had been given the task of forcing a breach in the lines of the 99th Infantry Division north of the Schnee Eifel through which his armour would flow. Peiper was exasperated when he discovered that this order hadn't been executed. As the day wore on *Kampfgruppe Peiper* remained practically inert. The main problem facing this advance was a destroyed railway overpass that hadn't been sufficiently repaired. It was late in the evening before Peiper finally managed to get underway via another route that wasn't really suitable for his heavy tanks. Peiper attempted to use alternative routes, one of which entailed driving through a German-laid minefield.

Kampfgruppe Peiper was used to fighting in the vast open spaces of the Russian plains where it was possible to manoeuvre. Peiper's unit was not designed to be confined to the narrow and constricting roads, small villages and towns.

By 17 December, the full force of this German attack was beginning to resonate all along the American lines as the SS units on the northern shoulder penetrated between the V and VIII Corps boundaries and finally managed to compromise some of their logistical problems. The German advantage in manpower, weapons, vehicles and numbers started to take its toll. In an attempt to control the twin villages of Rocherath-Krinkelt and forge a path to the high ground of Elsenborn ridge, the German 277th *Volksgrenadier* Division, supported by armour from the 12th SS Division, had made an assault against the lines of defence established by the US 99th and 2nd Infantry Divisions. If the Germans could control this region they would be capable of providing support to *Kampfgruppe Peiper*'s bid to reach the Meuse River. However, concerted resistance from these two US divisions prevented the Germans from achieving this objective. The 99th and 2nd had inadvertently stopped the German attack from reaching Liege, where a sizeable US ammunition and supply dump was located. There were additional US supply depots in Spa.

Heavily outnumbered five-to-one, the 99th held their positions and hit back with every ounce of strength they could muster. They pitted their brains against the raging brawn of the Germans and came out on top, but in the process they lost around 20 per cent of their effective strength, including 465 killed and 2,524 evacuated to the rear due to wounds, injuries, fatigue and weather-related maladies such as hypothermia and trench foot. They managed to inflict much higher casualties on the attacking Germans, killing roughly 4,000 and destroying 60 of their tanks.

To the south of the Elsenborn ridge, at 04:00 *Kampfgruppe Peiper* had steamrollered into the sleepy village of Honsfield, where they encountered one of the 99th Division's rest centres, congested with American troops and vehicles. Here resistance disintegrated quickly, allowing Peiper to push on to Bullingen where they destroyed some observation planes on the ground, and forced 50 Americans prisoners to refuel his vehicles with 50,000 US gallons of captured fuel. This was extremely valuable to *Kampfgruppe Peiper* because two fuel supply trains hadn't made it to the Losheim Gap on time. From there he followed a series of muddy byroads that ran through Mödersheid, Schopen and Ondenval to Thirlmont, which the 'spearhead' reached at noon. From there they should have continued straight west to Engelsdorf (now called Ligneuville), but in an attempt to get his unit back on track, Peiper had decided to make a detour to his initial trajectory and head north on the road that took him through the village of Waimes to the Malmedy–Vielsalm road that converged at the Baugnez crossroads. Making laborious progress, he then began to circumnavigate the eastern rim of the Amblève River valley and head south towards the village of Engelsdorf.

B Battery, 285th Field Artillery Observation Battalion, had been dispatched north from Malmedy. They had arrived there earlier that morning from Schevenhutte in Germany. As they headed north engineers felled trees behind them in an attempt to prevent any German columns hitting the town of Malmedy.

The 285th convoy had originally consisted of 26 vehicles, 18 trucks from the 285th FAOB (Field Artillery Observation Battalion), one ambulance from the 546th Ambulance Company, four ambulances from the 575th Ambulance Company and three trucks from the 68th Engineer Battalion. Among their number were two men of the 200th Field Artillery Battalion and 11 from the 32nd Armored Regiment, 3rd Armored Division. The convoy reached Malmedy at approximately 11:45. Four of the vehicles remained in Malmedy. The ensuing events have been debated, analysed, confirmed and refuted in innumerable publications. One book by Dutch-Flemish author Gerd Cuppens claimed that what occurred at the Baugnez crossroads on 17 December 1944 was a propaganda stunt by the Allies. It later transpired that Cuppens was an extreme right-wing fanatic who hated Americans. His version of the Malmedy massacre renders his so-called well-researched evidence null and void. He was biased and that tainted both his judgement and his account of the events.

Between 12 noon and 13:00 the main US column of 26 lightly-armed jeeps, command cars and trucks reached what the Americans called the '5 Points' crossroads at Baugnez roughly 4 km (2.5 miles) from Malmedy, where they turned right toward Sankt Vith. At the crossroads at Baugnez, the *Panzerspitze* (tank spearhead) of *Kampfgruppe Peiper* suddenly appeared, approaching the crossroads from the direction of Waimes.

Theodore Paluch was with the 285th FAOB. He was an avid 'Eagles' American football fan who lived in the centre of Philadelphia. More importantly, his account remained consistent throughout his life. The following is a transcript of his experiences recorded during a one-to-one interview in 2010.

'On 17 December we were in Schevenhutte, Germany, and got our orders to go. We were in the 1st Army; we got our orders to move to the 3rd Army. There was a tank column going with us, and they took the northern road and we took the southern road. That would have been something if they had gone with us south. Right before we left, a couple of guys got sick and a couple of trucks dropped out of the convoy, and they were never in the massacre. Also, there were about 15 sent ahead to give directions and all, and they escaped the massacre. From the massacre you saw guys, they got one guy named Talbert, I remember him, both arms, both legs, across the stomach. He lived to the next day.

'We had no idea that it was going to happen. We took a turn, like a "T" turn, and the Germans were coming the other way. We were pretty wide open for I guess maybe half a mile, and their artillery stopped our convoy. We just had trucks, and all we carried was carbines. We might have had a machine gun and a bazooka, but that was about it, we were observation. They stopped the convoy. We got out, and the ditches were close to five or six feet high because I know when I got in it, the road was right up to my eyes. There was a lot of firing, I don't know what we were firing at or who was firing at anything, but there were a lot of tracer bullets going across the road.

'Finally, a tank came down with the SS troopers behind it. They wore black, and on one collar they had a crossbones and skull and the other collar they had lightning. They just got us out, and we went up to the crossroad, and they just searched us there to get anything of value; cigarettes, and I had an extra pair of socks, and my watch, everything like that. They put us in the field there that was their front line; ours was two and a half miles away in Malmedy. Every truck and half-track that passed fired into the group, and why I didn't get hit too bad, I was in the front, right in the front, the first or second or third right in the front. Each track that came around the corner would fire right into the group in the middle so that they wouldn't miss anything, that's why I didn't get too badly hit. We laid there for about an hour, maybe two hours. While we were lying there, they come around, and anyone who was hurt, they just fired and would knock them off.

'Someone yelled, "Let's go!" and we took off. I went down the road there, there was a break in the hedgerow, and a German that was stationed there at that house came out and took a couple of shots at me, and I got hit in the hand. If he saw me or not I don't know, he went back and didn't fire at me anymore. I was watching him come, and there was a well, and I went over there. It was all covered up, and I laid down, and there was a little hill right behind where I was, and I just rolled. I got there, and I started coming in, and I got near a railroad, and I figured it would take us somewhere. I met a guy from my outfit, Bertera, and two other guys, one guy from the 2nd Division, he was shot, and another guy from the 2nd Division. The four of us came in together. It was dark when we got into Malmedy, but we could see some activity. I thought they would take us back, but they were on the move, so they could not afford to take us back.

'The first shots that were fired I laid down. I laid there after the tanks passed until someone yelled, "Let's go!" There were something like 75 who were killed right there. When we were captured and being brought up there, the people who lived there or in that general area brought up a basket. I guess it was bread or something, and they brought it up to them to eat. If I had been moaning, I would have been killed then.'

Just down the road from Baugnez in the sleepy village of Engelsdorf, amiable proprietor of the Hotel du Moulin, 69-year-old Peter Rupp, his wife Balbina, their daughter Maria and her two children, were preparing to go to Sunday morning service at the local church. Rupp was a fervent anti-Nazi whose son had been conscripted into the Wehrmacht. Although Peter was German by birth he was an active member of the Belgian underground organization 'The White Army', and had assisted the escapes of 22 downed Allied airmen during the German occupation. General Edward Wrenne Timberlake, commanding the 49th Anti-Aircraft Artillery Brigade, had set up an HQ at the hotel. At that time there was an impromptu collection of GIs in the village from various units and the Service Company of Combat Command B 14th Tank Battalion, 9th Armored Division, who were finishing off some maintenance work on a couple of tracked vehicles. The general along with most of the Americans had pulled out and headed south, leaving behind Captain Seymour Green and a handful of service company men.

That Sunday the pastoral calm was shattered when a bulldozer charged down the hill from the direction of Baugnez. The American driver stood up in his seat and shouted something about German tanks being on his tail. Standing in front of the hotel, Green immediately ordered his small outfit to prepare to move out. A Sherman tank adjacent to the Hotel du Moulin pointed its turret up the road and attempted to keep the Germans at bay, but within minutes it had taken a direct hit. Shortly after, forward units of *Kampgruppe Peiper*'s men arrived just as the first of Green's service trucks was preparing to leave.

From a kitchen window of his Hotel du Moulin, Rupp watched horrified as eight GIs were rounded up and herded into the courtyard of his hotel. A German NCO (non-commissioned officer) took his luger from its holster, placed the barrel in the mouth of one of the young GIs and pulled the trigger. A jet of blood, brains and skull fragments spurted from the back of the man's head as he slumped to the ground. Then the NCO moved to the next one and repeated the process. As the shots continued to resonate around the courtyard Rupp's eyes widened, he ran to the back door of the hotel and accosted the German: 'Murderer, they are prisoners of war, you have no right to...', the German savagely punched Rupp in the mouth, dislodging two teeth. One GI recoiled and attempted to run but the German seized him and executed him on the spot. A further 14 GIs including Captain Seymour Green were brought into the courtyard when another German officer approached and gave the instruction: 'Shoot them all, and the Belgian swine too.'

An officer wearing SS insignia heard Rupp's protests. He approached the assembled group and placed a hand on Rupp's shoulder. Then he instructed the German NCOs to treat the POWs as they themselves would expect to be treated by the Americans. They were led into a ground floor room of the hotel and placed under guard. The atmosphere was still volatile and, fearing that the killing could erupt again at any moment, Rupp sloped off to his cellar and returned with his arms full of quality cognac. He instructed his daughter to give a bottle to the guard so he could talk to the prisoners.

In the dark wood panelled room Captain Green asked Rupp if he was German or Belgian. Rupp replied that he was Belgian. Green thanked him profusely for the bottles and mentioned that his men hadn't eaten that day. This was the cue for Rupp to go to the kitchen and organize some food for the men. While he was in the process of bringing plates of food from the kitchen another SS officer accosted him and asked what he was doing. Rupp explained that the prisoners needed food. At that very moment Rupp's wife Balbina arrived and claimed barefaced to be a representative of the Red Cross. The SS officer believed her and grudgingly allowed Rupp to serve the food. Meanwhile, his daughter continued handing out five star cognac to other Germans, who drank rapaciously straight from the bottles. The lives of the remaining Americans had been saved. After the war General Eisenhower personally thanked Peter Rupp for his service and his timely intervention. Years later Captain Green would claim that it was Otto Skorzeny who interjected on behalf of the POWs, but this has never been conclusively proven.

Manfred Toon Thorn also passed through Baugnez and Engelsdorf that day. He was with the 1st SS Division, *Leibstandarte Adolf Hitler*. He wrote a whole book and even released a DVD titled *Mythos Malmedy* in which he claimed that the Malmedy Massacre never occurred. He said quite sternly, 'The Malmedy Massacre was a setup; it never happened. Those bodies were placed there by US intelligence to appear like they were all massacred. That is the end of it. December 17, 1944, we participated in the Ardennes Offensive ... Horst Pilarcek was our tank commander. He was two ranks higher than I was, and had not come from a tank unit and wasn't even an officer. Pilarcek saw an American column moving over the Baugnez crossing on the parallel road in the direction of Baugnez/Engelsdorf. Suddenly I heard my name as Pilarcek said, "Manfred, what should we do? I don't have any experience with these situations." I gave the "Fire" order to the gunner and we destroyed the first two vehicles of the moving column. The front of the column had already passed the crossing, and trucks coming up from behind crashed into the damaged vehicles. I could see no other damaged vehicles behind the trees and bushes from this distance, but I knew they were there. When we reached the crossing a few minutes later, we saw a scene of chaos.'

That morning *Kampfgruppe Peiper* had successfully navigated the Losheim Gap and headed out. Meanwhile, Dietrich's attacks in the north were succumbing to fierce American resistance. The notorious 1st Infantry Division (Big Red One) arrived on the scene and the 99th and 2nd Infantry Divisions withdrew to higher ground in proximity to the Elsenborn ridge.

At Malmedy, 84 prisoners of war were killed by their German captors. This version of events has been disputed by some historians, but the evidence points to the reality of the tragedy.

Peiper's situation didn't look too promising. Apart from the danger of losing momentum, he was now going to be confronted by elements of the 30th Division 'Old Hickory' that had been rushed from their reserve position to take the fight right to the SS. The 30th's 117th Infantry Regiment was heading south through Eupen and Spa, where they encountered columns of US vehicles moving in the opposite direction. General Bradley, meanwhile, had given orders to move General Courtney Hodges' 1st Army HQ south to Luxembourg. Bradley now fully comprehended that this was no minor enemy incursion; it was an all-out counter-attack by a determined enemy.

By 17 December many American outposts on the Schnee Eifel had been isolated for almost 24 long, arduous hours. They were all desperately in need of supplies. Unable to call in reserves and in some cases forced from the key positions which they had so staunchly been defending, they hung on. German infantry had infiltrated through the overextended US lines and repelled or captured some American artillery batteries, which deprived the encircled garrisons of desperately needed fire support. The situation of the 106th Infantry Division was becoming untenable. Poor communications between the infantry regiments and their HQ in Sankt Vith contributed to further confusion over what exactly to do next. The 422nd and 423rd were being bypassed. Many in the 422nd had not even fired a shot.

That same day, Albert Honowitz wrote: 'The chow jeep came around at three that afternoon. We knew they couldn't be bringing chow at that time. We soon found out. Our platoon Sgt., in the jeep, shouted to us, "March-order, fellas, the Germans are counter-attacking in Belgium, so we're going to Belgium." After the Major had told us that the Germans weren't expected to counter-attack, the whole affair seemed crazy to us. But we figured that it was only a minor counter-attack, and probably by the time we reach the trouble spot the Krauts would be already stopped.

'We hated to leave this good set-up we had had in that position, but we soon loaded our trailers, got in the column of B Battery's Half-tracks. For this mission there were altogether 12 AA tracks, 3 personnel carriers, a kitchen truck, a maintenance truck and jeeps. A total personnel of about 100 men. Four of the Battery's AA tracks weren't to go with us for this mission. B Battery, 796 AA, took off in column formation late that afternoon about 4 o'clock. We arrived in Luxembourg City about 8 or 9 o'clock that night. We slept in a former schoolhouse.'

Manteuffel's 5th Panzer Army had fought hard throughout the night to stay on schedule. Now they introduced tanks and were hitting the 424th Regiment with all their fury. The regiment was in a bad position with its back to the Our River. If the attacking German 62nd *Volksgrenadier* Division captured the only accessible bridge at Steinebrück, a retreat west would become impossible. Elements of the 62nd had incurred heavy casualties but were planning on driving out 1st Battalion, 424th Infantry. There had been some vicious hand-to-hand fighting as both sides struggled to dominate the position in the small village of Winterspelt. The 62nd *Volksgrenadier* Division had been unpleasantly surprised by the ferocity and determination of these fresh young GIs who didn't drop their weapons and run as predicted. The 106th artillery batteries A and B, 589th Battalion were approximately 1.6 km (1 mile) east of Schönburg on the Schönburg–Bleialf road. They had successfully retired to fresh positions, just before dawn when units of the 18th *Volksgrenadier* Division had captured Bleialf.

As the first hesitant rays of daylight permeated the dawn mist, a deuce-and-a-half truck from the battalion's Service Battery charged down the road to warn batteries that the Germans were right on his tail. Battalion executive Major Arthur C. Parker III took command and, thanks to a spate of clear, coherent thinking, he immediately ordered the remaining units of the 589th to move to new positions west of Sankt Vith. They would be safe for now at least.

About an hour after sunrise on the 17th, the fate of 9,000 men of the 106th Infantry Division was sealed. The grandson of western legend Buffalo Bill, William Cody Garlow was with the 423rd Regiment. General Alan Jones was particularly concerned about the developing situation because his son, Lieutenant Alan Jones, was also with the 423rd. American writer Kurt Vonnegut was also a private with the 423rd and was in the process of attempting to return to American lines. Exhausted, hungry, in serious danger of contracting hypothermia and down to a few rounds of ammunition, he and a few other soldiers huddled in a ditch by the roadside. They would soon be compelled to surrender.

Manteuffel had to move fast if he wanted to take the vital road and rail junction at Sankt Vith, which at that moment was defended by only 500 engineers, one infantry platoon and three anti-tank guns, but those young GIs out in Germany were putting up some serious resistance. They delayed the Germans long enough to allow the 7th Armored Division to reach Sankt Vith. This would become a game changer. Lead elements of the 7th Armored arrived in Sankt Vith at around 16:00, just one hour after German attacks had erupted a mile east of the town square. As the evening wore on, additional units of the 7th Armored arrived and were immediately thrown into the fray. Now that reinforcements had arrived on the scene to form a stronger defensive line, they guaranteed that Sankt Vith would not fall without a fight.

In the early evening of 17 December, 11 African-American artillerymen of the 333rd Field Artillery Battalion managed to extricate themselves from the Schnee Eifel and reach the tiny village of Wereth, just north-east of Sankt Vith. Two Belgian civilians, Mathias and Maria Langer, took the extremely precarious risk of bringing them into their home. According to the Langer story, a German sympathizer in the village informed on them. Sometime later, around 16:00, a four-man German patrol from *Kampfgruppe Knittel 3*, SS-PzAA1, 1st SS Division, arrived in Wereth in their *Schwimmwagen* (amphibious) vehicle.

At the time Langer took in the African-Americans he was also hiding two Belgian deserters from the German army and had recently sent a draft-age son into hiding to avoid conscription into the German army.

The SS soldiers approached the house, and within minutes the GIs surrendered peacefully. They were led out of the village to a small, muddy field. Over the next several hours, all 11 were inhumanly tortured, beaten and eventually shot or bayonetted to death. When their mutilated bodies were eventually discovered by a patrol from the 99th Infantry Division they saw evidence of horrific wounds and broken legs. Many had bayonet wounds to the head, skulls crushed. Some of the victims' fingers had been cut off. Army investigators were called to the site along with Signal Corps cameramen to record the grisly find. This war crime remained undocumented by the American military authorities and no one was ever prosecuted for it.

On the morning of that same day, 17 December, at the 10th Armored Division camp in Reméling, France, dishevelled GIs emerged from their tents into the brisk morning air. Raucous coughing, swearing and spitting accompanied their awakening as they surveyed the various forms of transport preparing to move north. Engines were filling the air with heavy exhaust fumes as they shuddered and lethargically groaned to life. M3 half-tracks, M4A1 Sherman tanks, and M10 and M18 tank destroyers all churned over the frozen earth like ploughs as they manoeuvred their way into the column that was preparing to move out. The 10th Armored Division had been ordered to assemble two combat teams, Combat Command A and Combat Command B respectively. Combat Command A would go to Echternach to provide armoured support for the 4th Infantry Division and Combat Command B were going to head up to Bastogne. 'We moved out in a column on 17 December. I know we travelled in the dark with headlights on, most unusual for lights to be on in a convoy in a combat area. I recalled it was raining, others say snowing,' said Don Nichols of C Company, 21st Tank Battalion, Combat Command B. 'The Tank Commander had his warm clothes on, as we all did, but he had his raincoat on, buttoned up to his neck and draped around the turret to keep the water from coming down on me and our equipment. We arrived in a city south of, or a suburb of, Luxembourg and were billeted in one front room of a couple's home. We slept on the floor. We listened to their radio to the BBC from London and they were playing big band music. It sounded great.'

The fighting that occurred on 17 December in the 4th Division sector down in Luxembourg was confined mainly to the 12th Infantry garrisoned areas, where the Germans forced inroads, but these penetrations were mild stabs, not deep cuts, and on most occasions they were driven back. The 12th Infantrymen had risen early that day to contact all isolated elements and attempt to restore previous outposts. By daybreak, the 22nd Infantry's regimental reserve was ordered to go to the 12th Infantry command post where they were joined by two tank platoons.

The opposing force was the 212th *Volksgrenadier* Division, part of Brandenberger's 7th Panzer Army. The 212th had spent three years on the Eastern Front. After being withdrawn from the Lithuanian sector in September they had been sent to Poland for urgent refitting and replacements. Many of their number hailed from Bavaria and a significant percentage were barely 17 years old. One of them was a young barber who got inadvertently captured by Private Emil Goss of the 76th Infantry Division. 'We moved in convoy into Luxembourg, and the soldiers in the 1st Battalion went into the line at Dickweiler, where they experienced the first taste of enemy fire. I had only been in a freezing foxhole for a few days when I accidentally took my first prisoner. He was a young German guy who had been a barber before the war. I took him back to our HQ, and he cut everyone's hair. Did a good job, too. We may have been cold and dirty and tired, but at least we had great haircuts.'

*Soldiers of the 45th Division,
1st Battalion await the Germans in
a foxhole in Niederbronn-les-Bains,
France, 10 December 1944.*

General Middleton was in a meeting with 10th Armored Division commander Major General William Morris Jr. at the VIII Corps HQ in Bastogne. So far Middleton had gauged the situation perfectly and used elements of the 9th Armored to provide a mobile defence force. Middleton placed great confidence in his subordinate commanders and encouraged teamwork while constantly searching for solutions to tactical problems. He had originally intended to use a part of the 10th Armored in direct support of the 28th Division, but instructed Morris to send one combat command to the Bastogne area and to commit the remainder of the 10th Armored to assist the 4th Infantry Division in Luxembourg. Middleton considered the German advance against the southern shoulder of his corps as potentially dangerous, both to the corps and to the command and communications centre at Luxembourg City. He didn't know at the time that Brandenberger only intended to head west as far as Mersch, 11 km (7 miles) north of the city.

Middleton's vast experience in holding terrain during critical times with limited resources allowed him to calmly direct the defence of Bastogne before the reinforcements arrived. His clear thinking and remarkable tactical acumen helped stall the German advance.

By 17 December the full magnitude of the German assault, and the breakthrough that should have occurred the previous day, began to take shape. Under cover of darkness Manteuffel's forward units surrounded key American positions and compromised their ability to provide direct artillery support, leaving infantry defenders vulnerable. Lead Panzer elements crossed the Our River in significant force and, by dusk, the majority of the 28th Division's defences in Marnach-Hosingen in the north of the Luxembourg area had crumbled. The 28th Division's 110th Regiment held on for dear life as Panzer grenadiers supported by tanks swarmed against their roadblocks. 'The smell of shit and cordite is what I remember,' said one GI of the 110th. 'We fired so hard that our fingers were freezing to the triggers, giving us blisters, but the thing I remember most is the smell. I reckon that a lot of our guys didn't wait for the order to evacuate.' The delaying actions of the 110th Regiment led to their inevitable annihilation, but purchased valuable time required to organize and reinforce the defences at Bastogne.

As the day ended on 17 December, US forces still held Sankt Vith and many of their battered units in the field were still putting up a serious fight. The German attacks on both the northern and southern shoulders hadn't gone exactly according to plan, and had stalled after making only nominal gains. After reviewing the situation after those first two days Rundstedt sent a message to Hitler with a recommendation to completely abandon the offensive and prepare to defend the areas already taken. Model deflected this idea completely, and suggested that the main weight of the attack should shift to Manteuffel's 5th Panzer Army in the centre where the most significant breakthroughs had occurred. In a rare conciliatory gesture, Hitler gave orders to redeploy two of Dietrich's SS Panzer divisions south to exploit Manteuffel's break-through, but the 6th Panzer Army would remain as the spearhead. For the Germans it was a matter of regaining the momentum in the north and south, and for the Americans it was a matter of digging in and holding on. Help was on the way but would it get where it needed to be in time?

Helping hands

18 DECEMBER WAS GOING TO prove a seminal day in the defence of the Ardennes sector. At his headquarters in Wiltz, Luxembourg, 28th Division commander and D-Day hero General Norman 'Dutch' Cota listened with growing consternation as scouts furnished him with disturbing reports from the front. Desperate attempts to resist the German onslaught were being made by his division who were mainly located along the Luxembourg–Germany border, but it was only a matter of time before the thin wall of resistance buckled and collapsed under the weight of this veritable tsunami.

On 18 December 1944, Albert Honowitz, B Battery, 796th Anti-aircraft Artillery Automatic Weapons Battalion, wrote: 'We were greatly impressed with the beauty of Luxembourg City, the smartly, well-dressed people. All the kids we talked to spoke English. The people were very friendly toward us. The seemed to know very little of a German counter-attack in Belgium. They made us feel that the entire counter-attack was being exaggerated. Their attitude reaffirmed my opinion that the Krauts would be stopped by the time we reached Belgium.

An anti-tank gun from the 7th Armored Division defends sets up a defensive position near Vielsalm.

In the Luxembourg town of Clervaux the situation was deteriorating by the hour. The town is in the pit of a valley surrounded on three sides by precipitous hills. Colonel Hurley Fuller called Cota early that morning from his besieged HQ at the Hotel Claravallis to request reinforcements. Cota initially rejected the request on the premise that he didn't have a clear picture of what was occurring at that moment, but after some discussion he agreed to send the 707th Tank Battalion. As the day wore on, only a limited number of the 707th's tanks made it to Clervaux where they were joined by a few 9th Armored Division tanks and some M10s from the 630th Tank Destroyer Battalion. Fuller's men were totally isolated, outnumbered and running low on ammunition. Clervaux had taken a hammering from elements of the German 2nd Panzer Division but it wasn't yet completely in German hands. Fuller's HQ was taking so many direct hits from German tanks and artillery that he decided to get the hell out of the building while it was still standing. Along with a few of his men, he made a frantic escape by climbing out of a second floor back window and then scaling a steep 50 m (164 ft) high hill directly behind the hotel.

'While we were still talking, one of the German tanks fired three rounds of cannon shells into the S-1 office in the room beneath me,' said Fuller. 'This fire came from a range of about fifteen yards, the tank being in the street in front of the CP. I asked the operator for HQ, 2nd Bn. While he was trying to get this connection, a blast of machine gun fire came from below through the window of the room I was in, knocking plaster off the ceiling over my head. I heard more tank firing outside, and then I was unable to get anything more out of the phone.'

Snow began falling heavily as the Germans infiltrated the town and became embroiled in vicious house-to-house fighting. Meanwhile, the chateau right in the very heart of the town was still held by around 50 GIs from the 110th's Headquarters Company. Fuller was a native of Texas and he compared the medieval Chateau in Clervaux to the Alamo. That comparison would be drawn with a number of other locations in the Ardennes before the fighting dissipated. Sergeant Frank A. Lo Vuolo, 'B' Battery, 107th Field Artillery Battalion, 28th Infantry Division, said, 'The only Americans remaining in Clervaux at that time were the dead and the captured. For them the war was over. Those of us who successfully made our way out of Clervaux eventually became part of an ever-growing stream of Americans moving west. There was mass confusion and I was a part of it.'

Further to the north, Manteuffel's 5th Panzer Army had surrounded most of the 106th Division's regiments on the Schnee Eifel and was approaching Sankt Vith from three directions. Five of his divisions had crossed the Our River, decimated the 28th Division and destroyed most of their roadblocks. Having eliminated most of the opposition, the infamous Panzer Lehr Division, one of Manteuffel's favourites, under the command of seasoned veteran General Fritz Bayerlein, began their advance along barely-navigable dirt tracks toward Bastogne. At the same time, most of the US 7th Armored were already providing support in and around Sankt Vith, and the 10th Armored Combat Command A had reached Echternach while their Combat Command B was heading with all haste to Bastogne.

In the south of Luxembourg, Brandenberger's 7th Army hadn't had much success. His remit was to protect the southern flank of the 5th Panzer Army's attack, cross the River Our and push forward on Manteuffel's south. He was charged with the additional task of preventing Patton's 3rd Army from striking north to Bastogne. During those first two days the 7th had only penetrated 8 km (5 miles) into the Allied line and were in danger of being driven back across the Sauer River. Brandenberger had a total of four *Volksgrenadier* divisions at his disposal that were organized into two corps. Whereas the 4th Infantry Division now had armoured support from the 10th Armored Division's Combat Command A, Brandenberger didn't have any Panzer regiments at his behest.

Kampfgruppe Peiper had reached the town of Stavelot late the previous evening, on 17 December. Peiper complained bitterly that he had been forced to use roads that were 'unfit for tanks and even bicycles'. He was behind schedule, but after three continuous days of travelling and fighting his unit was completely exhausted. Owing to the poor condition of the roads, *Kampfgruppe Peiper* had created a 20 km (12 mile) tailback and its Tiger battalion had been forced to use a more accessible road further south. It didn't re-join the *Kampfgruppe* until late on the 17th, whereupon it took position on a hill just above Stavelot. If the crucial bridge over the river Amblève could be crossed at Stavelot on the 18th the *Kampfgruppe* would have an open road to Trois Ponts and Stoumont, which would bring it in close proximity to the Meuse River.

At this juncture, Peiper took the command decision to pause for the night to give his men and himself some much needed rest. The next day they would wreak havoc. Many years later Peiper explained the reasons why he stopped at Stavelot. 'At 16:00 we reached the area of Stavelot, which was heavily defended. We could observe heavy traffic moving from Malmedy towards Stavelot, and Stavelot itself seemed clogged up completely with several hundred trucks. That night we attempted to capture Stavelot but the terrain presented great difficulties. There was a short curve just at the entrance to Stavelot where several Sherman tanks and anti-tank guns were zeroed in. Since I did not yet have sufficient infantry, I decided to wait for the arrival of more infantry.'

Kampfgruppe Peiper were part of Sepp Dietrich's 6th Panzer Army and Dietrich was already claiming to have achieved the furthest incursion into the Allied line. He was referring to *Kampfgruppe Peiper* reaching the perimeter of Stavelot. He omitted to add that his other columns had only managed to advance a few kilometres, and this fact hadn't gone unnoticed at Hitler's HQ, where the subject was already causing great consternation.

In spite of his generally slow progress, Dietrich insisted he was on the verge of achieving a resounding victory. One of his subordinates observed that, 'The butcher's son can't walk or talk straight and he smells like shit.' Despite his detractors, when he commanded the 1st SS and I SS Panzer Corps Dietrich retained a paternal approach to his subordinates. Every time he sent his soldiers into combat he always gave the same instruction: 'bring my boys back'. Whether or not he would actually be able to see them if they came back is another matter entirely.

'We were aware that we were not making the progress we should have been. Although we still had some fuel and our supply lines weren't that long, there was an atmosphere of desperation about it all. We didn't know that the whole 6th Army effort was faltering and had been for a few days,' said Erwin Kressman, 6th Panzer Army, Heavy Panzer Brigade 519. 'I was a Jagdpanzer driver. I just drove my Jagdpanzer and did my duty as expected. Conditions were very cold, but I had experienced much worse on the Russian front in the east. In comparison, this wasn't so bad. Constant strafing by Yabos [P-47 Thunderbolts] didn't help the situation, though. I fought mostly in Germany around Nideggen, where I'd been during the Battle of the Hürtgen Forest. A couple of months later, I was awarded a Knight's Cross and given a courage vacation by the army. I'd earned it.'

Kampfgruppe Peiper's SS officers synchronizing their watches. Timing was everything during the Battle of the Bulge.

The primary objective of Manteuffel's 5th Panzer Army was to cross the Meuse River at Dinant before the Allies could destroy the bridges. His original plan did not entail taking Bastogne, but the strategic significance of this city had been acknowledged by both the German high command and SHAEF. Manteuffel had doubtless the most favourable terrain, which was the most conducive to tank and troop manoeuvre. Moreover, he was a seasoned tactician who had learned from the best. He had meticulously studied maps of the region and understood the topography perfectly, but regarded Bastogne as a city that would have to be contained, not necessarily taken. It would transpire that some of his subordinates had other ideas on the subject.

The Allies recognized the importance of Bastogne. The previous day Eisenhower had released the two available airborne divisions being held in reserve in France and sent them towards the Ardennes. The troops were hurriedly loaded into M35 open-topped port battalion trucks, which were normally used for transporting tanks. The weather was already beginning to turn colder and snow had been forecast as Ralph K. Manley of the 501st Parachute Infantry Regiment, 101st Airborne Division, that had been earmarked to go north, remembered: 'I was in Paris on a 24-hour pass after we just returned from Holland, and a loudspeaker came on saying, "All units report to your units immediately, as quickly as possible, any way possible." So, we returned then from Paris back to our unit and immediately got on what clothes we had. I still had on my class A, of course, for being in Paris, and we loaded onto port battalion trucks, these semi-trucks that had four-foot sidewalls on them and open tops, loaded onto those without overcoats and without overshoes and headed toward the Bulge, and it was very cold.'

Both airborne divisions were ill-provisioned at all levels. Brigadier General McAuliffe had placed the 501st Parachute infantry regiment (PIR) at the head of the column and driven on ahead to meet General Middleton in Bastogne. The 82nd Airborne Division had initially been chosen to go to Bastogne but was behind the 101st, so Middleton made the tactically sound decision of dispatching the 82nd to Werbomont, where they would keep an unscheduled appointment to meet *Kampfgruppe Peiper*, and attempt to prevent Peiper's move to reach the Meuse River. Werbomont was, and still is, a small farming community at the western end of the Amblève valley.

By the early morning of 18 December, the 30th Division's 117th Infantry Regiment had reached their assembly area at Malmedy at the eastern tip of the Amblève valley. This ancient Ardennes town still has a twin-spired church at its centre and is surrounded by steep, wooded hills on three sides. The 30th Division's men heard a broadcast from 'Axis Sally' reported on German radio: 'The 30th Infantry Division, the elite Roosevelt's SS Troops and Butchers, are en route from Aachen to Spa and Malmedy, Belgium, to try to save the 1st Army Headquarters, which is trying to retreat from the area, before they are captured by our nice young German boys. You guys of the 30th Division might as well give up now, unless you want to join your comrades of the 1st Army HQ in a POW [prisoner of war] camp. We have already captured most of the 106th Division, and have already taken Sankt Vith and Malmedy, and the next will be Liege.'

Axis Sally, real name Mildred Gillars, was an American citizen who had moved to Berlin in 1934. She was born on 29 November 1900, in Portland, Maine; she died on 25 June 1988, in Columbus, Ohio. During World War II she became a notorious enemy radio broadcaster. When they could tune in, Axis Sally broadcasts from Berlin entertained Allied troops. She had a very sexy voice and an excellent inventory of popular American music, which was interspersed with ersatz intelligence reports. 'Good morning, Yankees. This is Axis Sally with the tunes that you like to hear and a warm welcome from Radio Berlin.' In 1949, Mildred Gillars was tried on eight counts of treasonable conduct, but convicted of just one, which was sufficient to get her incarcerated until 1961. Her radio broadcasts were intended to spread discontent and disillusion among the ranks, but they were largely unsuccessful. There is no record of any Allied soldier being charged for desertion because they'd listened to Axis Sally, but she was by all accounts highly entertaining and had great taste in music.

'We got on trucks and headed south. We were in a convoy travelling at night, without headlights. Sometimes we had a guy walking out in front of the truck so we wouldn't crash into the truck in front of us. While going down to the Bulge the guys were listening to Axis Sally on the radio,' said Hank Stairs, HQ Company, 17th Infantry Regiment. 'She [Axis Sally] said the 30th Division was heading south and would be annihilated by the German counter-offensive. She also referred to us as Roosevelt's SS troops. Jerry flew over us and dropped a few bombs, but he didn't know where he was dropping them. We stopped and someone shouted, "Bail out and get down!" We never fastened our helmet chinstrap and I wore GI glasses at the time, so my helmet came crashing down on my glasses and sliced open the bridge of my nose. That was my only chance for a Purple Heart! We reached a town called Malmedy and stopped there. I think the 117th was the first regiment to get into the town. The Germans hadn't taken it yet and the Air Corps didn't know it and they bombed us, again! I thanked God we survived.'

On the cobbled road between Stavelot and Trois Ponts, the Mignon family had heard the distant booms of artillery and gunfire. The father had moved some cushions and pillows into the basement and attempted to make it as cosy as possible for his three young daughters and his wife. They had survived four long years of Nazi occupation and were terrified that these evil Germans were going to return.

Despite the ferocity of the combat during those first few days of the Battle of the Bulge, there were surprisingly few desertions on the Allied side. Life on the front lines for the Allies had taken its toll both physically and mentally. Between June 1944 and April 1945 the US army's Criminal Investigation Division (CID) handled a total of 7,912 cases. Forty per cent involved misappropriation of US supplies. The rest were cases of violence, rape, murder and manslaughter. But desertion was also a serious problem for all the Allied armies in Europe. Private Eddie Slovik, Company G, 109th Infantry Regiment, 28th Infantry Division General, was the only US serviceman to be executed for desertion in World War II. He was strapped to a post in a farmyard at Sainte-Marie-aux-Mines, France, and executed by 12 riflemen who were all members of the 109th Infantry Regiment. In later years, Slovik's wife petitioned the US government for posthumous clemency for her husband. It was never granted. Slovik was just one of 102 US service personnel executed by military authorities during World War II. He was, however, the *only* American soldier to be shot for desertion; the other condemned men were put to death for committing, and being found guilty of, either rape or murder.

Over 40,000 American and nearly 100,000 British soldiers abandoned their posts during the war and were listed as having deserted. The German army was much tougher on deserters. The Wehrmacht executed some 15,000 soldiers for desertion during World War II. Today, these men are remembered in Germany as victims of war.

In retrospect, the number of German army executions pales by comparison with Mother Russia's record. More than 158,000 Soviet soldiers were summarily executed for abandoning their posts during the war. Others were sent to penal battalions, which was basically the equivalent of a death sentence. Unauthorized retreats were not recommended in the Soviet Red Army. To prevent this from happening during combat, Stalin ordered the formation of what he pertinently called 'blocking detachments'. These units usually had a few machine guns and would be strategically positioned just behind the front line to shoot down any soldiers that attempted to run away. Stalin once remarked: 'It takes a very brave man to be a coward in the Red Army.'

One individual who definitely would not have been tried for desertion was Ernest Hemingway, who appeared to have nurtured an almost psychotic obsession with war and death. He was in Paris recuperating from a bad case of pneumonia when the fighting in the Ardennes began. On hearing the news he immediately got out of his bed and headed to Belgium. Although ostensibly a journalist, he ripped the correspondent's badge off his uniform, leaving only the four green ivy leaves of the 4th Infantry Division's shoulder patch. He impressed professional soldiers not only as a man of courage in battle but also as a genuine specialist in military matters, guerrilla activities and intelligence collection. There were even rumours that he worked as a spy during World War II.

He made his way to Luxembourg, met up with his friend Colonel Buck Lanham, and insisted on re-joining the 22nd Regiment, 4th Infantry Division, but was in such bad condition physically that Lanham immediately handed him over to the regimental physician, who put his famous patient to bed with a massive dose of sulfa drugs. That December Hemingway reluctantly retired to the town of St Hubert, comfortably away from the fighting.

During the fighting in the Hürtgen Forest when Lanham had ordered him to take cover, Hemingway ignored the request point blank. 'You're as safe in one place as you are in another under artillery fire unless you're being shot at personally,' Hemingway remonstrated. 'Besides, if you hear a shell coming ahead of time, it won't hit you.' A sketch artist who was present at the scene said, 'Hemingway's behaviour was both impressive and insane.'

In the meantime, on 18 December Hemingway's favourite division, the 4th, were feeling confident. Their general, 'Tubby' Barton, decided that it was time to order a counter-attack. On hearing this news, as soon as units from 10th Armored Division's Combat Command A arrived in the 12th Infantry sector, the 'Ivy' men (the Ivy name came from the roman numeral IV) immediately went up to the line to grab a piece of the action. The plan was that supporting armour from Combat Command A would advance in three task forces. The first one, Task Force Chamberlain (led by Lt. Col. Thomas C. Chamberlain), would advance on the left flank; then in the centre Task Force Standish (commanded by Lt. Col. Miles L. Standish) was dispatched to assist the 2nd Battalion, 12th Infantry, while Task Force Riley (under Lt. Col. J. R. Riley) would go to cover the right flank and head towards the town of Echternach. Some of Brandenberger's infantrymen were attacking with estimated company strength, but this attack was successfully repulsed and the Germans were compelled to resort to harassing the defenders with long-range artillery. When the 12th Infantry's 3rd Battalion organized a successful supply mission to Echternach, the balance finally tipped in favour of the 4th Infantry Division.

CHAPTER TEN

Waves of hate

SOME TIME DURING THE NIGHT of 17–18 December, Peiper reorganized his *kampfgruppe*. He dispatched two companies, equipped with Mk IV tanks, to secure the Amblève River bridges at Trois Ponts and then advance to the Meuse River using the southern route. Then Peiper made preparations to take the vital bridge over the Amblève River at Stavelot. What he didn't know was that at 02:00 a small American task force comprising A Company, 526th Armored Infantry, and the 1st Platoon of A Company, 825th Tank Destroyer Battalion, had arrived in Stavelot. At the time of their arrival there was only one American unit in the town. C Company of the 202nd Engineers, VIII Corps, equipped with 20 mines and one bazooka, set up a roadblock at Stavelot. Their commander, Lieutenant Joe F. Chinland, had failed to blow the Stavelot bridge as ordered, but had laid the mines there and placed a platoon with a machine gun to cover it with two other platoons to the north of the bridge in defensive positions around the town square. Chinland and his men hadn't slept a wink that long night. They knew that those vehicles and men assembling on the hill above Stavelot were SS.

'My company C was sitting in Stavelot, Belgium, with orders to defend the town,' said Carl C. Miller, a 202nd Engineers veteran. 'The shelling started just before daybreak and I was walking to chow with Russ Beamer. He and I left for the Army together and went all through the war together. I asked Russ, "Do you think we will ever see Carroll County again?" He replied, "Carl, it doesn't look very good now." The fight was continued from early morning until just before noon.'

The 526th Armored Infantry Battalion had 3 in (7.6 cm) anti-tank guns, which they used to reinforce the engineers' roadblock. When the first attack came, the Armored Infantry managed to repulse the SS, but was no match for the guns on German tanks that began to menacingly roll toward the bridge. All American units on the Bulge would be deeply grateful for the presence of their engineer battalions before the fighting was over. These engineers were brave, resourceful and equipped to do the job.

At 08:00 the engines of around 800 vehicles belonging to *Kampfgruppe Peiper* roared into life and commenced their attack on the bridge. They were rested, revived and ready to wreak havoc. For the defenders and the unwitting inhabitants of the sleepy little town of Stavelot there would have been no more terrifying prospect than being in the path of 1st SS Division's *Kampfgruppe Peiper*. These were not reluctant amateurs forced into the fray against their will. These were experienced Waffen-SS, ice cold, resolute killers who knew their jobs. Their method of fighting was both brutal and merciless. They would give no quarter and God forbid anyone who dared to get in their way. They would murder anything with a pulse, age and gender no object.

The men of the 30th Infantry Division had faced off against the 1st SS division before and they knew what to expect. They could match them man for man and gun for gun. Stavelot was recognized as a key enemy objective for two specific reasons. First, there was an excellent bridge on the south side of town over the Amblève River. Second, two road networks to Liege converged just west of Stavelot. If Peiper could reach these he would have access to the fuel depot in Liege and open ground to the north and west of that city. This made attacking his combat unit an imperative for the 30th and there was no time to waste.

Before daybreak two M10 tank destroyers of the 825th had positioned themselves on high ground about 250 m (820 ft) north of the river where they could clearly observe the German column assembled along the road waiting to take the bridge and storm through the town of Stavelot. SS mortars and artillery protecting the Panzers' advance rained down on the American defenders. The tank destroyers zeroed several German Panzers and released their first rounds. A couple of the German tanks appeared to take direct hits and began to smoulder. In the heat of battle none of the Americans were sure whether it was the M10s or one of the three US 57 mm (2.5 in) anti-tank guns that disabled the first two tanks. A split second later, the dreaded German 88s retaliated. One anti-tank gun and its crew evaporated while one managed to escape. The third anti-tank gun continued firing until it was just 35 m (115 ft) from its target then it was inevitably forced back over the river.

'The Americans had committed all the heavy weapons available in Stavelot to protect this bridge. Several of our Panzers lost a few feathers here. Worse was the fact that one of our Panzers was hit and blocked the narrow bridge access,' said Karl Wortmann, a Flakpanzer commander. A fierce firefight ensued as lead elements of the *kampfgruppe* seeped across the bridge and began rolling through Stavelot. Eventually, the firing dissipated and Peiper's men began heading out west in the direction of Trois Ponts.

In response to the German advance, between midnight and dawn on 18 December, American reinforcements were hastily dispatched to the Malmedy–Stavelot area. The 291st Engineer Combat Battalion quickly reinforced the 2nd Battalion of the 117th Infantry Regiment. They dug in side by side along the embankment of the railroad that ran between Malmedy and Stavelot before setting demolition charges on the viaducts and laying minefields on all the approach roads that converged just outside the town.

All the footbridges that crossed the Amblève River in that sector had already been blown to rubble. As *Kampfgruppe Peiper* traversed through Stavelot it became a harrowing battleground where men of the 1st Battalion of the 117th ducked and dodged between exploding masonry to avoid being blown to pieces by the German tanks that were holding out there. The town square became a ghastly no-man's-land littered with dead and dying soldiers from both sides. SS men brutally kicked in doors and sprayed houses with machine guns while rolling potato masher grenades through cellar windows. Peiper would later claim, 'When we penetrated Stavelot, too many civilians shot at us from the windows and openings in their roofs. The only goal that I was looking for was the bridge near Trois Ponts. I, therefore, had no time to spend on those civilians and continued driving on, although I knew that resistance in this town had not been decisively broken.' Other men from his unit said that local civilians were concealing GIs in their homes.

An American lieutenant who was in Stavelot with the 526th said, 'The Germans brought in these massive King Tiger tanks, that's when the shit really started to fly. Our peashooters had no chance against those fucking metal monsters.' A request for reinforcements was made at 09:00, but the small American unit was unable to reach their HQ. Half an hour later they were told to evacuate the town. As Peiper headed west through Stavelot, the town eventually became divided between the two forces, with Americans to the north and Germans to the south, and that would remain the case for the next few weeks.

US 117th Infantry sent in squads supported by M-10s from the 843rd Tank Destroyer Battalion to begin counter-attacking Stavelot in Peiper's wake. As evening descended on the 18th roughly half of the town had been recaptured.

Terrified by the sound of approaching vehicles, 11-year-old Arlette Mignon huddled close to her sisters in the cellar of a small house on the road between Stavelot and Trois Ponts. She said, 'SS soldiers from *Kampfgruppe Peiper* burst into our cellar where I was hiding with my mother and father and two sisters. Someone pushed open the door and began firing. I felt a pain like a punch in my leg, the pain was terrible but I was too afraid to scream. I thought that I had wet myself but it wasn't urine, it was a lot of blood running down my legs and making a small pool beside me. The man left and I turned to my sisters. The youngest one had been shot in the face. They shot and killed my mother and my two sisters who were younger than me.' Arlette took a machine gun bullet to her thigh, and since that day in December 1944 she has never cried or displayed any outward emotion of any kind. There were many other civilian casualties.

Monique Thonon claimed to have been killed three times by Peiper's SS men. She was 23 months old at the time, and she lived in the sleepy hamlet of Parfonderuy close to the city of Stavelot. A member of Peiper's *kampfgruppe* killed her mother and shot Monique in the legs. Covered in blood, she was left for dead. A little later the SS gathered the bodies of their victims together and Monique's limp body was thrown on to the pile. Then an SS man, who has never been identified, poured petrol

Arlette Mignon was in the cellar of a small house on the road between Stavelot and Trois Ponts when the SS burst in. They killed her mother and her two sisters.

(they didn't have much to spare) on the bodies. Just as he was about to ignite the pyre a blizzard blew in and he gave up on the job.

By 11:00 lead elements of the *kampfgruppe* were tenuously approaching the town of Trois Ponts, regarded as a crucial bottleneck. It's the town where the Amblève and Salm rivers converge. But while fog still clung to the east and south of the Ardennes, the skies there in the area between Werbomont and Stavelot were clear enough to launch an Allied air attack. During the afternoon of 18 December, 16 P-47 fighter-bombers flew under the low clouds to strafe Peiper's column as it laboriously headed west. This was just one of the many obstacles that Peiper would have to contend with as he pushed west. The P-47, nicknamed the 'Jug' (short for 'Juggernaut') by adoring pilots, was a heavyweight war bird that packed a devastating punch. They swooped low and inflicted serious damage on *Kampfgruppe Peiper*'s column that extended almost 23 km (14 miles) all the way back to Bullingen. This made his men and machines a relatively easy target for the experienced P-47 pilots, one of whom described the experience as a 'turkey shoot'.

Peiper was already experiencing fuel problems and was completely unaware that, as he headed to Trois Ponts, just 1.5 km (1 mile) north of Stavelot, on the Francorchamps road, there was a sizeable US fuel dump there for the taking. When Major Paul Solis, acting CO (Commanding Officer) of the 526th Armored Infantry Battalion, arrived on the scene he ordered the Belgian guards to dig a shallow trench across the road and fill it with as much fuel as they could. This was promptly ignited, whereupon it produced clouds of dense black smoke. Solis considered this to be the perfect anti-tank barrier, but it served no purpose because Peiper remained completely ignorant of the fact. He was fanatically focused on his objective. But his worst fears would soon be realized.

CHAPTER ELEVEN
Teamwork!

THE WEATHER REPORT FOR SOUTH Belgium issued by the London Meteorological Office for Monday, 18 December 1944, forecast dense fog and intermittent light snow showers with a mild north-easterly wind. The expected temperature was -11°C.

A major strength of the US army in World War II was their remarkable capacity to be able to divide units up into small autonomous teams as the situation demanded. While 10th Armored Division's Combat Command A were providing excellent support for the 4th Infantry Division down in Luxembourg, Combat Command B was heading with all haste to Bastogne. Combat Command B was divided into three teams, each with a specific predetermined objective. Middleton determined that Manteuffel's 5th Panzer Army was advancing in the direction of Bastogne from the north, north-east and east of Bastogne on the main approaches to the city. The purpose of the Combat Command B was to establish defensive blocking positions to hinder or prevent the advancing enemy forces from capturing this key city, with specific instructions from Middleton to 'hold at all costs'.

Major William Desobry gallantly led Team Desobry. He was severely wounded in the bitter fight against the German 2nd Panzer at Noville.

Colonel Roberts, commanding the 10th Armored Division, met with General Middleton at his VIII Corps HQ in Bastogne. They studiously reviewed the emerging situation and decided where to allocate the teams. 'Sir, there will inevitably be stragglers,' Roberts said. 'I want your permission to use these men.' The corps commander immediately acquiesced.

As the evening blanketed the landscape of 18 December, Roberts met the vanguard of his column 1.5 km (1 mile) south of Bastogne. Roberts trusted his old friend Middleton implicitly; he had served with him in World War I and been his classmate at the US Army's Leavenworth military college.

As each team filed past, Roberts issued Middleton's instructions. Team Cherry at the head of the column commanded by Lieutenant Colonel Henry T. Cherry Jr. were ordered to head north-east to cover the approach to Longvilly. Team O'Hara, commanded by Lt. Col. James (Smiling Jim) O'Hara, were assigned a sector along the Bastogne–Wiltz road to prepare for an assault from the east. Team Desobry, commanded by the young, gangly Major William Desobry, Commanding Officer of the 20th Armored Infantry Battalion, 10th Armored Division, was sent to Noville a few kilometres north of Bastogne.

'We got into Noville around midnight and we got the first call after midnight that the enemy was coming down the road and they fired on the outpost,' said Jerry Goolkasian, who served with B Co. 3rd Tank Battalion, part of Team Desobry. 'This was the first connection with the Germans around the area of Bastogne on the night of the 18th. The Germans pulled back because they believed they had run into a bigger force than what they had. The half-track behind us got hit and that was flaring up all night. Ziggy, my driver, and I got some .50 calibre ammunition from the burning half-track because we were desperate for ammunition.'

Another 'Tankie' complained about having spent 14 hours straight in the cab of his M4 Sherman. 'We'd all eaten something bad down in France and we're all griping about having the shits. Problem was that we were on the move and couldn't stop to get out and take a dump. The smell inside the cab was indescribable, but once the Krauts started hitting us we quickly forgot. Worst fucking time of my life I can tell you.'

While 10th Armored teams braced for the impending attacks and began to anchor their teams in their designated locations, Team Desobry's column snaked north towards Noville. Desobry's advance guard, including an intelligence and reconnaissance platoon, 20th AIB (Armored Infantry Battalion), and a section of 1st Platoon, Troop D, 90th Cavalry Recon Squadron, arrived in Noville at around 22:00. They reported that there wasn't any immediate enemy activity apart from the occasional lone vehicle that had drifted in from areas already overrun by Axis forces. Lacking precise knowledge of the nature of the enemy forces or the direction from which they would come, Major Desobry decided to establish three outposts on the ridges that were situated roughly 1 km (0.6 miles) to the north and north-east of the centre of Noville. Each outpost was comprised of a section of medium tanks and a platoon of armoured infantry.

With the 101st Airborne commander General Maxwell Taylor back in Washington DC attending a conference, Brigadier General Anthony McAuliffe assumed command of the division. The 'Screaming Eagles' were originally designated to go to Werbomont on the northern shoulder to check the advance of the SS in that sector, but were redirected to Bastogne when the 82nd Airborne got ahead of them on the road north through Luxembourg. McAuliffe immediately went to VIII Corps headquarters in Bastogne to talk with Middleton.

Phil Burge of C Company, 55th Armored Engineer Battalion, said, 'When we arrived at 101st Airborne's headquarters I saw General McAuliffe, a one-star general at the time, chewing out some paratrooper who apparently was not in proper uniform. It was something about the tie or neckerchief he was wearing. Who is this guy? I thought.'

Robert Kinser was a combat medic with the 3rd Tank Battalion assigned to Team Desobry. He remembered: 'We rolled into Bastogne, it was pitch black and we could not even see the next vehicle. We were to go to the next town but found out it was filled up so we stopped at Bastogne for the night. We had no idea how far the front was.' The sheer magnitude of trucks that managed to get troops to the Ardennes was staggering, but herein lay the strength of the Allies in the ETO. From 17 December over 11,000 trucks moving 60,000 men and supplies headed to the Ardennes sector. It was a logistical masterpiece that managed to transport over 250,000 Americans within the space of a week. One haggard and exhausted driver pulled over to the side of the road to catch up on some sleep. He was rudely awakened by an MP (military policeman) banging his M1 carbine on the truck door and shouting, 'Get your ass in gear you lazy fuck, the Krauts could be here any minute.' 'Well I hope they fucking get you first, you miserable sonofabitch,' the driver riposted.

The lead elements of the 101st Airborne Division reached Bastogne late on 18 December and their timing couldn't have been better. During the night of 18–19 December the German advance had progressed rapidly down the Wiltz–Bastogne road to within 3 km (1.8 miles) of the city. When Middleton prepared to leave for his new headquarters the following morning he met McAuliffe and said, 'Hold Bastogne.'

As the 101st began to arrive in significant numbers they received orders to take up positions mainly in support of the 10th Armored teams. As they trudged up to their designated locations they saw haggard and terrified stragglers arriving down the approach roads. Many of the paratroopers accosted these men and attempted to relieve them of any weapons they were carrying. Paul Bebout of the 101st said, 'We had nothing with us, no warm winter clothing, not enough weapons so we had no choice back then, we had to bum these things off the guys that were falling back.' A company of paratroopers from the 1st Battalion, 506th, commanded by Lt. LaPrade, were ordered up to Noville to provide support for Team Desobry. When LaPrade arrived at the headquarters in Noville, Major Desobry and LaPrade had a slight altercation regarding command. This detail would shortly become superfluous.

Phil Burge saw paratroopers from the 101st Airborne Division marching in to Bastogne. 'They had come in by truck, since it was impossible to drop them in by air. Eventually the whole division of the 101st Airborne was in Bastogne. But we were there first, by a matter of hours.'

On the northern shoulder, men of the 30th Infantry Division were preparing to take on the SS again and hopefully turn them back. These 'Old Hickory' men were tough veterans that had seen plenty of action in Normandy and Aachen. They had earned the unofficial title 'Rock of Mortain', because of their heroic defence of that town against the 1st Division SS and other German units. They were often supported in combat by the 3rd Armored Division, and that would be the case again. Combat Command B of the 3rd Armored Division organized three task forces with the order to go immediately to the assistance of the 30th Division. The largest of these was Task Force Lovelady, led by Lieutenant Colonel William B. Lovelady, which was organized around the 2nd Battalion, 33rd Armored Regiment and attached units. The other task forces of Combat Command B were Task Force McGeorge (Major K. T. McGeorge) and Task Force Jordan (Captain John W. Jordan). Task Force McGeorge was designated to drive south from La Reid, attack La Gleize, and pass through elements of the 30th Division. Task Force Jordan would take Stoumont while the primary objective was handed to the largest of the three task forces, Task Force Lovelady. It was to clear the road from La Gleize to Stoumont, while Task Force Jordan would take the town and then turn east to join Task Force McGeorge in La Gleize.

Before these task forces arrived on the scene *Kampfgruppe Peiper* was becoming increasingly frustrated by the antics of the American engineer units who were intent on encumbering Peiper's progress. Trois Ponts was held by a small number of these engineers who blew the main bridge just before Peiper arrived on the scene. He was approaching the town from the north bank of the Amblève from Stavelot, while a smaller column moved simultaneously along the south bank towards the high ground at Wanne. This route converged to the south of Trois Ponts, where another bridge crossed the Salm River.

Trois Ponts was the location of the HQ of the 1111th Engineer Combat Group. One of its units, the 291st Engineer Combat Battalion, had detachments operating throughout the region. The 51st, also part of the 1111th Combat Group, received orders to defend Trois Ponts and prepare all the bridges for demolition. While the 291st wired the bridge over the Salm River, Company C, reinforced by an anti-tank gun and a squad of armoured infantry, prepared other defences. As soon as Peiper's tanks were noticed on the turn in the road that led under the railway bridge, a powerful explosion announced that the engineers had blown the main bridge.

'We came upon the railroad; the order "sharp left" came over the radio. At that moment we were hit, but, thank God, it was only a graze. Apparently, we were moving too fast,' recalled Eugen Zimmermann, one of Peiper's tank commanders on point. 'I was able to exactly recognize the anti-tank gun and aimed the cannon directly through the barrel, at a stone wall immediately behind the anti-tank gun. One high-explosive shell and there was no more resistance. We cautiously negotiated the underpass. I thought for sure there would be another anti-tank gun. It was quiet! But the bridge on the left was blown.'

The Amblève River was shallow enough for infantry to cross at Trois Ponts, but owing to the steep banks it remained a formidable barrier to vehicles. While Peiper dispatched a detachment of German tanks to find an alternative bridge, the main body of his column waited impatiently on the east side of the river. Peiper's intention had been to hit Trois Ponts, but after discovering that the bridges there had been destroyed he recalculated his route and decided to head north towards La Gleize on a road that runs almost parallel to the Amblève River. Just west of there he planned to cross the Amblève, continue through Cheneux, and rejoin the Werbomont road east of the Lienne creek. His other option was to continue along the Amblève through to Stoumont. While Peiper decided to follow the creek to Cheneux, his Mk IV companies that had branched off at Stavelot took the option of continuing along the Stoumont road to the west of La Gleize.

With a hard day's fighting behind him, and darkness descending accompanied by dense mist, Peiper looked down the road, past the lead tanks of his Panzer column and towards the small wooden bridge at Neufmoulin that crossed the Lienne creek on the road to Habiemont. This hadn't been his intended trajectory but his options were decreasing by the hour.

The high hills that ran parallel to the creek had incited Peiper to become more cautious. He was confined to the road he was on and there was no feasible alternative. This wasn't 'tank' country. Standing in the cupola of his tank, he impatiently grabbed his binoculars and peered tenuously again towards the bridge. This time he noticed a few mist-silhouetted figures rushing across the bridge to the opposite bank. '*Verdammt*' Peiper sneered through clenched teeth as he realized what was transpiring before his eyes. The column's lead Panzer opened fire with its hull-mounted machine gun and, within seconds, the whole front of the Panzer column was pouring machine gun bullets and tracers at the bridge.

Then Peiper's face registered a sardonic smile because now he assumed the only resistance between his armoured vanguard and Habiemont was this small, seemingly innocuous group of American infantry recoiling into the shadows under the weight of fire. 1,134 kg (2,500 lb) of TNT caused a deafening explosion that quickly wiped the smile from Peiper's face. All that remained of the bridge was a distended pile of fractured timber and rubble. The team of engineers had severed yet another route to the Meuse River. Unable to supress his increasing frustration, Peiper hammered the hull of his tank and allegedly spat out the memorable words, '*Diese verdammten ingenieure!*' ('These damned engineers'). While the explosion still rang in his ears, Peiper shook his head. The objective of reaching the Meuse River was slipping further from his grasp. From that point on his situation would continue to deteriorate. The bridge had been blown by Company A, 291st Combat Engineer Battalion, led by Lieutenant Alvin Edelstein. A few kilometres up the road at Werbomont the 82nd Airborne were arriving in force, and within hours they would be confronting Peiper and taking the fight to the SS.

In the sleepy hamlet of Neufmoulin, Pfc Mason Armstrong, an expert bazooka man from Company F, 119th Infantry Regiment, peered into the gloom from the upstairs window of a roadside house. Three German half-tracks carrying soldiers from SS-Panzer-Grenadier Regiment 2 approached the roadblock in the dark. As they turned the sharp corner, 35 m (115 ft) from the roadblock, the lead vehicle turned on its lights. Mason Armstrong had positioned himself well, with a machine gunner on the second floor. From this vantage point he managed to accurately aim three shots as a group of three half-tracks full of German infantry began to ascend the hill. The machine gunner who gave Armstrong cover was killed after one of the half-tracks fired at the house. Armstrong survived and managed to take out two of the half-tracks and disable the third. This singular action effectively blocked one of the only roads that led to Werbomont. The house where he fired his bazooka is still there. Peiper left a rearguard and most of his anti-aircraft units at Cheneux and decided to return to the main road that ran through Stoumont. First, he gathered his forces in and around the village of La Gleize. After studying maps of the area he made his move. Time and fuel was running out for Jochen Peiper and his team.

Pfc Mason Armstrong, F Company, 119th Regiment, 30th Infantry Division stopped a whole column of SS in Neufmoulin. He was awarded a DSC for his bravery.

CHAPTER TWELVE
A foggy day

TEAM DESOBRY EXPERIENCED ONE OF the most significant and vicious encounters of the whole battle for Bastogne in the small village of Noville, which looks pretty much the same today as it did back then in 1944. This team consisted of 15 medium tanks, five light tanks, a company of infantry transported in M3 half-tracks and a platoon of five M10 tank destroyers. A unit of mechanized cavalry in three armoured cars and six Willy's jeeps also accompanied them. After establishing the roadblock, taking up positions on the ridges, and after repelling a few minor probing enemy incursions, Team Desobry prepared for the main attack. Throughout the night American engineers attempted to install minefields in support of Desobry's roadblocks but discovered that it was impractical to obey this order due to the interminable flow of American stragglers from the 9th Armored Division's Combat Command R along with men from the 28th Infantry Division falling back west to escape the advancing German divisions on these same roads. Colonel Roberts had instructed Major Desobry to draft them into his organization along with any other strays.

Roberts ordered the ones that made it back to Bastogne to be assembled into what he described as a 'strategic reserve' with the igno-minious-sounding name of 'Team SNAFU' (Situation Normal all-fucked-up).

During the night of 18–19 December, Team Desobry's Captain Geiger established roadblocks on the Vaux, Bourcy and Houffalize roads, the three main approach roads that converged on Noville, and placed a slender screen of infantry just beyond the main buildings. One tank was sent to cover the southern Bastogne road and two were placed on the other main exits from the town. Artillery support was provided by a 57 mm (.25 in) gun and a 75 mm (3 in) assault gun. The action opened with a group of German half-tracks belonging to the 2nd Panzer Division looming menacingly out of the gloom and fog at 05:30 on 19 December. Due to the poor visibility, GIs manning an outpost on the Bourcy road that converged on Noville couldn't determine whether they were friend or foe. In an attempt to determine the identity of the approaching vehicles a GI sentry shouted 'Halt!' four times. The first half-track stopped a few metres from the outpost. Suddenly a voice in the half-track shouted out something in German. That was the timely cue for Desobry's men to shower it with hand grenades. Several exploded as they landed inside the stationary vehicle. The blast was quickly followed by agonized, almost feral howls of pain and derision as spouts of blood and severed limbs ejected into the freezing air. Some bloodied and broken survivors attempted to crawl out but were immediately dispatched by the GIs. The rest of the enemy column quickly dismounted and deployed in the ditches that ran parallel to the road. A close-quarter fight ensued for around 20 minutes as the opposing forces hammered away with grenades and automatic weapons.

Greatly outnumbered, the roadblock sentries managed to take cover behind an earthen embankment that absorbed most of the enemy's bullets. Around the same time, Desobry decided that his own vehicles were congesting the village. He ordered the main streets to be cleared and the vehicles to be parked along the side roads. Detailing one officer to stand watch, he then suggested that the rest of the force within the village try to snatch a few hours' shut-eye, but there was going to be no time to sleep. On 19 December, long before daybreak, the flow of American stragglers abruptly ceased and Desobry's men flexed in prepa-ration for the impending German attack.

Around the same time, Team Cherry, commanded by the stoic Patton admirer Lt. Col. Henry T. Cherry, had arrived in Longvilly, roughly 12 km (7.5 miles) east of Bastogne. Getting past the column of 9th Armored and remnants of 28th Division heading west was problematic and disconcerting for the small team as they approached their destination. While Team O'Hara set up their positions to the south-east in Bras, Colonel Roberts established his Command Post at the Hotel Lebrun just a few yards from the main square (Place McAuliffe), which was then known as the *Carrefour* (the Square). These teams, supported by three batteries of the 420th Field Artillery Battalion, were the first line of defence until reinforcements from the 101st Airborne arrived. The rest of the 10th Armored Division was held back in Luxembourg providing vital assistance to the 4th Infantry Division and hoping to prevent the Germans from swinging into Bastogne from the south.

On 19 December 1944, Albert Honowitz wrote: 'Woke up about 9:00 that morning, went down the street where the kitchen was set up, ate a pretty good breakfast there at Battery CP. All the boys eating chow talked about the possibility that the fact of being cut off might be true. None of the boys firmly believed that we were severed from American lines, though. When I got back from chow I found that the half-tracks had been dispersed, so that in case of an air raid one bomb won't knock them all out. Our track had been moved next to a house set off from the other houses on that block about 30 feet from the house I had slept in. That morning we found that we were attached to CCB [Combat Command B] of the 10th Armored Div. CCB had reached Bastogne about one hour before us.

'We had our eggs so we decided to go back to our half-track. We shouldn't have left the track in the first place, as a particular mission may have come up while we were gone. The remainder of the crew would have no alternative but to take off and leave us behind. We were halfway back when we saw a blonde waving at us from her doorsteps. We waved back. We didn't want to go over to her as we had been away from our track over an hour now. We made motions with our hands that we'd come back at 6 o'clock that nite. She understood the 6 o'clock motion and yelled back laughingly, "O.K."

'We came back that nite at 6 on the dot. The blonde introduced herself and the family. None of them understood English including the blonde, and we couldn't speak Belgian. But all of us soon understood the sound of German shells crashing in the street. Blackie and I took off with the family to the cellar. In the cellar we noticed that it couldn't have been

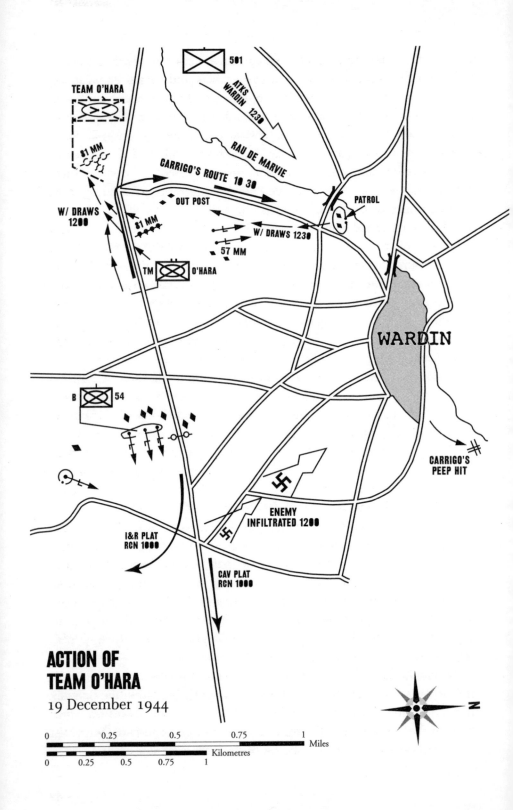

501

ATKS
WARDIN 1230

TEAM O'HARA

81 MM

RAU DE MARVIE

CARRIGO'S ROUTE 10 30

OUT POST

PATROL

W/ DRAWS
1200

81 MM

W/ DRAWS 1230

57 MM

TM   O'HARA

WARDIN

B   54

CARRIGO'S
PEEP HIT

ENEMY
INFILTRATED 1200

I&R PLAT
RCN 1000

CAV PLAT
RCN 1000

ACTION OF
TEAM O'HARA

19 December 1944

0   0.25   0.5   0.75   1
                                    Miles
                    Kilometres
0   0.25   0.5   0.75   1

N

the first time the family had been forced to seek shelter in the cellar. The cellar had already been set up with tables and chairs. The shelling lasted for 15 minutes. We then bid adieu and went back to our half-track. That nite I decided to sleep at the house where our half-track was parked. The occupants were an old French-speaking couple. They had been accepting us in their house all day long to wash and warm up. I slept in their kitchen as it was warmer than the other rooms. The old couple slept in the attic, as they had just about forced the other fellas to take their bedroom downstairs.

'This old couple were real characters. The Germans shelling and closing in on the town didn't seem to worry them the least. The old woman claimed that when the Germans first captured the town in 1940 they marched into her house, stole her only clock from the wall, tore off the cupboard and oven with their missing doors. She made a little curtain in place of the missing cupboard door. It made me feel that to innocent old people as they, everything said about the ruthlessness of the German soldier was without a doubt true.'

Newly-appointed 2nd Panzer Division commander Colonel Meinrad von Lauchert decided to up the momentum and gave the order to unleash his artillery against Team Desobry's positions in Noville. Determined to get off the barely passable side roads that he had chosen to circumnavigate Bastogne, he attempted to blast his way battering ram-style through to the west of Noville. Hitler had specified that if Bastogne couldn't be taken quickly then it should be bypassed. The German attack was already behind schedule and time was of the essence.

Twenty minutes after the fighting had dissipated on the Bourcy road near Noville, three tanks approached the outpost on the Houffalize road. Staff Sergeant Major I. Jones was in a foxhole about 60 m (196 ft) in front of the roadblock. As the tanks closed on his position, Jones fired a quick burst with his Browning Automatic Rifle (BAR) over the turret of the lead tank. Suddenly fire from one of the tank's machine guns opened up and he flattened as the bullets whizzed over his head. This was the cue for men at the roadblock to return fire.

Suddenly, amid the pandemonium, a cry of 'Cease-fire, they're friendly troops!' was heard. Due to the all-consuming fog Jones couldn't ascertain if the order had come from the force in front of him or from his own lines to the rear. The small-arms exchange abruptly stopped. One of the two medium tanks, which were supporting the roadblock about 100 m

(328 ft) from the approaching armour, opened up with its 75 mm (3 in) gun. The first round hit the roadside bank 15 m (50 ft) from Jones and almost blew him out of his foxhole. The opposing lead tank replied with six rounds in quick succession. The first round disabled the American tank on the right. The second round eliminated the other one. Remarkably, none of the American tankers were killed but several were badly injured. One man slumped from the hull of his tank with his right leg blown off and his left dangling by a bit of muscle and sinew. Private John J. Garry crawled out of the ditch to assist the wounded tankers. 'Don't move. I'm coming to get you buddy,' he shouted. Moments later he was hit in the shoulder by a sizeable piece of shrapnel.

Meanwhile, Jones and the other men in the advanced positions were pinned down in their foxholes by the raking fire from enemy guns. American half-tracks in line behind the destroyed tanks prevented the enemy from gaining access to the main road, and provided cover so that they could turn their machine guns on the approaching enemy column. A bazooka team tried to get forward but couldn't find a route by which they could bring their rockets to bear. Under these conditions of deadlock the two forces continued to hammer it out head-to-head, while the fog swirled around them and eventually closed in so thick that they could scarcely see the muzzle flashes from their own guns.

At 07:30 the platoon disengaged and withdrew back to the perimeter of Noville. Acting on Desobry's orders they had held until the last minute and fully complied, but it was a timely withdrawal because their ammunition was almost spent and enemy infantry were approaching around the flank. The Vaux roadblock didn't get attacked at that juncture but they distinctly heard the ominous grumble of approaching German armour.

From Noville's main street the north road runs straight for miles to the town of Houffalize. The defenders assumed that they were drawing fire from German tanks but were unaware of their proximity or exact location. The sustained fire destroyed three half-tracks and a jeep and catapulted the machine gun from an M8 car. At around 08:30 two Tiger tanks loomed out of the dense fog and drew to a shuddering halt within 20 m (65 ft) of the American machine-gun positions covering the northern sector. The machine gunners that saw this occurring immediately grabbed their bazookas and fired simultaneously. Within moments the Tigers had been hit and disabled. As surviving crew members bailed, the German infantry following in the wake of these tanks recoiled and disappeared back into the fog.

An hour later the attacking forces began to bear down on the western approach to Noville with a series of sporadic probing actions. Second Lieutenant Eugene E. Todd felt that the whole German army was hitting his positions. Feeling the full weight of the enemy, he requested permission to withdraw. Captain Geiger replied, 'Hell, hold your ground and fight.' Todd didn't have any other option. At 11:00 the fog cleared temporarily but the sight that met the Americans who were manning the foxholes and dugouts was a sobering experience. It began to dawn on the team that they were taking on a whole German Panzer division.

'We went through Bastogne, and then the little town of Foy, and then we got outside of Noville,' said Walter Lepinski, HQ Co., 20th Armored Infantry Battalion. 'In my company I was always the last vehicle in our column, and the column stopped. I heard a German plane, an Me 109, evidently a reconnaissance plane, all the sudden I heard a pop and it was a gosh darn flare and it lit everything up like the daylight as it dropped down slowly. I said to myself "Dammit, we are going to get a lot of artillery on us." But I did not hear any firing, and it was getting dark fast. After the flare faded, word was passed back to me from half-track to half-track that Captain Geiger wanted me to come forward and report to him. That is how I got the message, we did not use radios. I moved forward to report to Captain Geiger, who said to me that he and I were going to go into town and pick the spots to place the platoons and gun positions. Captain Geiger and I left the platoon and walked into the town, it was not very far, and after we passed the first house, which was on the left-hand side of the road, we went into town and walked around the area. Once he decided where to place each platoon he called the column to move up to the town. I asked Captain Geiger, "Captain, in the case of a withdrawal, what is the alternate route back out?" He said to me, "Our orders are to stay here and battle to the last man." My heart dropped. At that point there was no firing, small arms or artillery, it seemed so strange. It continued to get dark. I was there with him as he placed each company into positions and I got my men into their position as well. That night my men and I slept on the floor of this schoolhouse that we found on the left side of the town. I didn't know it was a schoolhouse until I saw the desks there. I was tired as all hell and I slept.'

A platoon from the 609th Tank Destroyer Battalion drove into Noville, to provide additional firepower as a violent exchange of bullets and shells ensued for the next 30 minutes. Fully aware that his situation was becoming increasingly precarious, Desobry contacted Colonel Roberts at his HQ on the Route du March in Bastogne and asked to withdraw from his current position. Initially, Roberts vehemently rejected this request but he later instructed Desobry to 'trust his own judgement'.

'The next day, we spotted three tanks on the horizon on the road towards Vaux, the junction that met the main road at Noville. Hildoer, he was a good shot, fired the 75 mm [3 in], and shot four rounds out there and the fourth round caused the tank to stop. The other two tanks surprising enough turned sideways and with one shot we stopped the second one, and with two more shots we stopped the third one,' said Jerry Goolkasian, Company B, 3rd Tank Battalion. 'A half-track came down the road, after Captain Schulze congratulated us after taking out the German tanks, so we hopped into our tank and obliterated it. I was concerned naturally with the amount of shells being fired, it was never ending. The 101st came up around noon, we saw them walk up the road and we turned our turret around because we were told not to be expecting any more ammunition or fuel. This fact did not make us feel too well because we assumed we were going to be surrounded. We turned our turret around because we were not expecting any reinforcements. We knew they were American paratroopers because we trained at Fort Benning at the same time as they did. The 101st dug in around us, and the shelling continued the rest of the day into the night.'

As the fog drew in again one GI fired a quick burst with his BAR over the turret of an approaching tracked vehicle that came to a halt about 20 m (65 ft) from his foxhole. He heard the occupants conversing in English. Then fire from the tank's .30 calibre broke around the foxhole, only missing the heads of the three occupants by inches. Suddenly a cry went up of 'Cease fire, cease fire, they're friendly troops!' The GI shouted: 'I wish this goddam fog would lift and give us a clear view of those heinie bastards. This is starting to seriously piss me off.'

Then German fire started up again in earnest and before long the GIs were pinned in their foxhole. Across the road two damaged US half-tracks that were in line behind some destroyed Shermans had reinforced the roadblock. The position of the ruined tanks not only prevented the enemy from coming down the road but also allowed the half-tracks to turn their .50 calibre machine guns against the approaching enemy column. Under these deadlocked conditions the two forces continued to slug it out almost face-to-face while the fog swirled around them and at last closed in so thick that they could scarcely see the muzzle flashes of their guns.

Desobry was heartened by the arrival later that morning of the 1st Battalion of Colonel Robert L. Sink's 506th Parachute Infantry Regiment, that were going to prove integral to repulsing the increasingly powerful German attacks. They even managed to launch a temporary counter-attack before digging in around Noville.

Further back down the road across from one of the main buildings, a medic approached a wounded GI and surveyed the physical damage with utter disbelief. The man had lost both his legs below the knee and his right arm was no more than a bleeding engorged stump. Surprisingly, he was still conscious enough to beg the medic to finish him off but the medic refused this request and began to administer a phial of morphine to the man's thigh. Suddenly the wounded man used his one good arm to whip a grenade from his belt and extracted the pin with his teeth. The medic dived away just in time to see the body disintegrate in a small cloud of torn flesh and blood that slapped down on to the cold road like fresh meat on a butcher's block.

Major William R. Desobry, 20th Armored Infantry, Silver Star citation:

'On 19 December 1944, in the vicinity of Noville, Belgium, he was in command of an armored task force composed of tanks, infantry, tank destroyers, assault guns and mortars with the mission of holding the village at all cost. At daylight the first of a series of strong enemy attacks with armour and infantry was delivered and repulsed, as were all other attacks. After and during each attack, Major Desobry exhibited gallantry and good judgment in reorganizing and disposing his forces to meet attacks from any direction. His outstanding leadership and unerring sense of duty under heavy enemy fire encouraged the men serving under him to greater efforts in the performance of an arduous duty. During an attack by the enemy he was seriously wounded and evacuated. The personal bravery, tenacity of purpose and fortitude displayed by Major Desobry were in accordance with the highest standards of the military service. Entered military service from New York.'

Major William Desobry, 20th Armored Infantry Battalion, 10th Armored Division wrote: 'When they hit the building they really took it down. And they killed LaPrade, I guess probably ten to 12 guys, and I was badly wounded, hit in the face, head and the eyes. The guys took me down into the cellar and when I came to they told me I was badly wounded and the doctor said that I had to go back to the hospital. So I said, "Well, I want to go back and talk to Colonel Roberts, the Combat Commander," because I was convinced that we couldn't stay in Noville, and we had to get back on that ridgeline at Foy where we could do a much better job. But I wanted to go back and tell him. He hadn't come up to see us. The only ones that would come up to see us during the day were General Higgins from the 101st and Colonel [Robert F.] Sink, the [506th Parachute Infantry Regiment] regimental commander, nobody from the 10th Armored. They knew what the situation was and they had agreed with us that we ought to go back to Foy. They didn't have the authority to say that, though. So, I wanted to go back and see Roberts and so I asked that they get my jeep and take me back there and so the jeep driver went out to get the jeep and he never came back.'

At 18:00 an 88 mm (3.5 in) shell had hit Team Desobry's command post and immobilized both the infantry and the armoured commanders. Lieutenant Colonel LaPrade was killed outright, and Major Desobry was wounded. His face was covered in lacerations and the percussion from the blast had forced his left eye out of its socket on to his blood-striped cheek. After his visit to Col. Roberts he was taken to the 326th Medical Clearing Station. The timing couldn't have been worse.

Captain Doctor Jacob Pearl, 326th Airborne Medical Company, escaped from the Division Clearing Station when it was overrun and wrote the following statement: 'At approximately 22:30, 19 December 1944, an enemy force estimated at six (6) armored vehicles consisting of half-tracks and tanks, supported by one hundred (100) infantry soldiers proceeding southwest from the direction of Houffalize, Belgium, on route N26 attacked the Division Clearing Station of the 326th Airborne Medical Company. The Division Clearing Station was sprayed by machine-gun from the half-tracks for a period of approximately fifteen minutes. The tents in which medical treatment was being carried out [were] struck by the machine-gun fire. Six (6) division trucks were set afire and lighted the area so that the red crosses on the Division Clearing Station tents were visible to the enemy. Machine-gun fire continued after the trucks were burning and after the nature of the installation was visible to the enemy. Following cessation of machine-gun fire an enemy officer approached the station and questioned Lt. Colonel David Gold, Division Surgeon, the senior officer present. After a discussion with the enemy officer, the Colonel surrendered the 326th Airborne Medical Company to the enemy. The enemy allowed the organization thirty minutes to load the equipment and personnel on the vehicles and then carried them back to the German lines.'

Desobry was among the wounded at the 326th clearing station. He spent the rest of war in captivity. Hospitalized by the Germans at Ibbenburen, Germany, he was later transferred to Falingbostel, Germany, a branch of the Belsen prison camp, and was liberated in the spring of 1945. Major Robert F. Harwick, executive officer, 1st Battalion, 506th PIR, assumed command of the combined force; Major Charles L. Hustead took over the armour. The fight at Noville proved to be an excellent delaying action that further frustrated the German schedules. Despite the odds of around 10-to-1 in favour of the Germans, Team Desobry had stopped the whole 2nd German Panzer Division and destroyed 31 enemy tanks in two days of hard fighting. Captain Jack Prior, a doctor assigned to the 20th AIB, courageously volunteered to stay behind with some of the wounded, fully aware that he would probably be taken prisoner along with his wounded patients. At the last minute as German armour was entering the village and only yards away from his aid station, he managed to load the remainder of his wounded soldiers on a half-track to get back to Bastogne in one piece, but the fight was still on.

In an effort to get through to Bastogne, on 19 December at around 07:00 General Bayerlein launched his Panzer Lehr Division against Team Cherry. The chateau that Col. Cherry had established as his CP was under attack from three sides and eventually caught fire. Despite this, Cherry refused to abandon his post until the late evening. As the hours passed paratroopers from the 101st consolidated Team Cherry's positions and continued repelling attacks made by the Panzer Lehr. American artillery further frustrated German attempts to head west by zeroing shells on all roads leading to Bastogne from that area.

On 20 December, German artillery began raining down on Team O'Hara's positions south of Wardin. The previous day had seen a vicious running battle during which fog had effectively masked all observation. Fearing that an infantry assault was imminent, O'Hara's men hit out with every gun and mortar that they could bring to bear on the Germans.

*American soldiers from the
289th Regiment marching to cut
off the Sankt Vith–Houffalize road,
24 January 1945.*

At 11:00 the supporting 2nd Battalion, 327th Glider Infantry, in Marvie also began to receive concentrated enemy artillery fire and had observed enemy tanks moving toward them. Team Hustead (previously Team Desobry) had run the gauntlet to get back to Bastogne. Team O'Hara had so far failed to stop the interminable flow of German troops and vehicles heading westward, and Team Cherry could no longer tackle the approaching enemy. It was time to retire to safer positions closer to the perimeter of Bastogne.

Out on the Schnee Eifel, young Jim Cooley of 423rd regiment, 106th Infantry Division, was spending his final moments as a free man. 'So we fought there until the morning of December 19th, then we got orders to fight our way out. I guess we were about five miles behind German lines, maybe more. At this time the Germans shelled us, and I got wounded in my left upper arm. I was lucky, of course, during the shelling. I was lying flat on my stomach, and I had my arms over my head. I was lucky it hit my arm instead of my face or something, or going into some other part of my body. So, a medic came by in the afternoon and cut off my sleeve and gave me a shot of morphine. But we were out there in the cold, and it was really cold, and on the battlefield and bleeding for the rest of the day. This was also December 19th. About 17:30 or 18:00 that afternoon or night the officers decided to give up. So we destroyed what weapons we had and we gave up.

'To show the intensity of the battle, I'll kind of go up the line. My captain, Captain Clarkson, was killed. My battalion commander, a lieutenant colonel, was killed. And I'd say we had about, oh, 35 per cent casualties in our outfit. Anyway, I was captured and I was marched. I don't know, of course, but the body does wonderful things when you have something happen to it. You reach the point where you're just numb. They marched me into kind of a, not a hospital, just a barn where German medics were working on wounded people. I stayed there a day; two days, something like that. The German medics wouldn't look at any Americans. They would look at Germans regardless, and if they got through with Germans, they would start on us. Finally, they took me in and poked around with a needle to find the shrapnel or whatever was in there and could not find it.'

A few days later Jim Cooley was put on a cattle truck and taken to a stalag in Germany where he would spend the rest of the war. He was indeed one of the first American foot soldiers to cross the Rhine River.

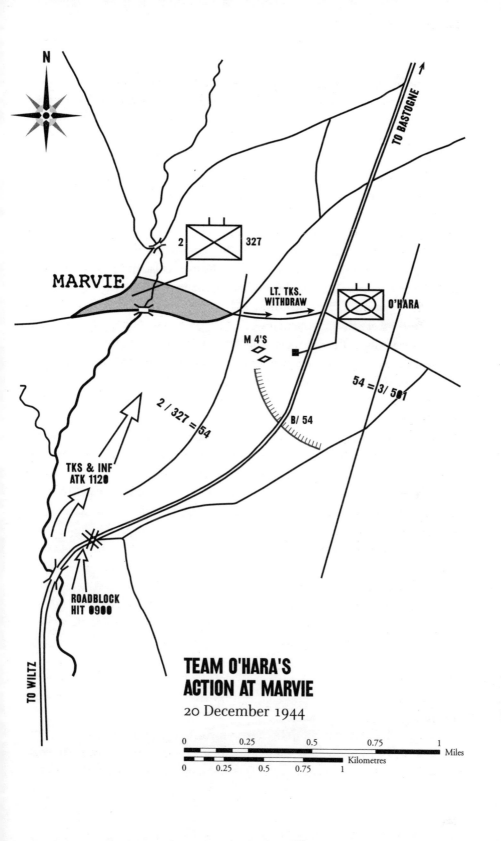

N

MARVIE

2 ⊠ 327

LT. TKS.
WITHDRAW

⊗ O'HARA

M 4'S

TO BASTOGNE

54 = 3/ 501

2 / 327 = 54

B/ 54

TKS & INF
ATK 1120

ROADBLOCK
HIT 0900

TO WILTZ

**TEAM O'HARA'S
ACTION AT MARVIE**
20 December 1944

| 0 | 0.25 | 0.5 | 0.75 | 1 |
Miles

Kilometres

| 0 | 0.25 | 0.5 | 0.75 | 1 |

General McAuliffe had his final meeting with General Middleton on 20 December at Middleton's newly established VIII Corps HQ in Neufchateau. They discussed the current situation at some length and, as Middleton left, his parting famous addendum to McAuliffe was: 'Don't get yourself surrounded, Tony.' Approximately 11,000 airborne troops and auxiliaries had made it to Bastogne and they were going to be integral to the defence of that city, but their task would have been considerably more difficult without the assistance of the 10th Armored Division's Combat Command B and artillery units that proved invaluable.

German intelligence had assessed the situation prior to the offensive considerably better than their counterparts, but had erroneously assumed that the 101st and 82nd Airborne Divisions were preparing for another airborne operation. They didn't predict that US forces would make a concerted effort to hold Bastogne.

The fighting on the northern and southern shoulders had not gone according to plan. The Germans attacked the 4th Division sector in Luxembourg with prescience of both its strength and dispositions, but when the plan was put into operation, the German 7th Panzer Army was seemingly reluctant to take full advantage of this prior knowledge. Consequently, although the 4th endured a hard fight it wasn't greatly afflicted or affected by German intelligence, which had also greatly underestimated the US forces' capacity to enact rapid, decisive operational factors and evolve as the situation demanded. Herein lay the true strength of the US forces in the ETO in 1944.

CHAPTER THIRTEEN

Seven roads

THE COMBAT COMMAND B ROADBLOCKS were all beginning to buckle under the sustained weight of German attacks. In an attempt to gauge an accurate picture of the developing situation, American jeeps, trucks and half-tracks sped along the seven frozen approach roads to Bastogne to and from the battle lines. One of the jeeps doing recon near Team O'Hara's positions near Wardin and Marvie to the west of Bastogne contained an illustrious Broadway actor and relative of Hollywood legend Lionel Barrymore, 1st Lieutenant John Drew Devereaux.

Devereaux and his driver, O'Hara's second in command, S2 Captain Edward Carrigo, emerged from the dense fog and cautiously approached the village of Wardin. As they arrived at the centre of the village, Carrigo pulled over to the side of the road. A few wary villagers abandoned the safety of their cellars and approached the two Americans. As the villagers convened around the jeep, Lt. Devereaux, who never missed an opportunity to perform, vaulted athletically out of the vehicle and stood bolt upright on the bonnet of the jeep and with a dip of his eyebrow and a small pout on his lips began to address the assembled hosts. 'Have no fear good people,' he said, 'the United States army is here to stay and we shall protect you.' He concluded his little performance with a low, theatrical Jacobean bow as his ad hoc audience, mightily impressed, cheered, waved and even attempted to embrace the theatrically-satiated actor, who smiled benignly and tapped Carrigo on the shoulder.

Carrigo stubbed out his cigarette and rolled his eyes: 'Wanna take the wheel?' 'They love me,' replied Devereaux. 'Yeah, so does Uncle Sam, now let's get moving.' With the sound of his audience still ringing in his ears, Devereaux and Carrigo drove east back into the fog, in the opposite direction from whence they came. Suddenly their attention was diverted by the sound of approaching heavy engines. A shell burst into their intended path followed by a burst of machine gun fire. The two Americans looked at each other in astonishment as muzzle flashes punctuated the grey gloom and machine gun bullets now tore up the ground around the jeep. Then they began to discern the silhouette of an approaching vehicle but couldn't ascertain whether it was American or German until they heard the voices.

'My God they're Krauts,' exclaimed Devereaux, wrenching the gear lever into reverse and pressing the pedal to the metal plus momentum. Within seconds they were whizzing back through Wardin at full speed with Devereaux shouting to the locals, 'Get out of the way you morons the Krauts are coming!' A little while later the two officers were reporting their findings to a bemused Lieutenant Colonel James O'Hara. He listened assiduously as Carrigo described the recent events before turning his attention to Devereaux. 'Lay off the theatricals for the time being, son,' he said, then placed a paternal hand on Devereaux's shoulder. 'It's distracting for the locals.'

His men knew Lt. Col. O'Hara as 'Smiling Jim', because no matter how serious the situation was he always sported a beaming toothy grin. Some of his men did indeed find this attribute reassuring while others found it downright disconcerting.

The people of Bastogne are known as *Les Bastognards*, and they are a special breed. Tenacious, generous and stoic, they were no strangers to conflict, but this time it was different. After the first German bomb had impacted close to the St Peter church on the main street they had taken to congregating in private and communal cellars. One of these cellars was beneath the Notre Dame school a few hundred yards up the road from the church. During the bitter fight for Bastogne it became the only refuge for more than 600 civilians, and around 50 nuns. As bombs and ear-shattering explosions impacted in close proximity to the cellar, clouds of asphyxiating dust shook loose from the ancient rafters, combined with acrid pungent tobacco smoke that rendered the air in the cellar almost unbreathable. This vast subterranean space was illuminated only by sparse candles and narrow shafts of light that occasionally pervaded the murkiness below. With water and electricity supplies disconnected, sanitation was provided by buckets that quickly filled up and overflowed as temperatures plummeted below zero.

Incessant, resonant screams of panicking children intermingled with the agonized, derisive wails and moans of the wounded and dying provided an interminable calamitous drone that would have tested the resilience of even the sturdiest observers. One of them was a young nurse who had returned home to Bastogne to spend Christmas with her father and aunt. Augusta Chiwy had arrived in Bastogne on 16 December.

With its meagre population of just 9,000, Bastogne became a focal point of the German attack. Around two-thirds of Bastogne's citizens had already fled the city. Augusta Chiwy volunteered to help care for those confined in the sprawling cellar beneath the Notre Dame school. She would later volunteer on two more occasions to assist in caring for wounded GIs under the auspices of 20th AIB medic Dr John 'Jack' Prior.

As the perimeter around Bastogne contracted American soldiers and civilians adopted a siege mentality. The weather report for south Belgium from the London Meteorological Office, for Wednesday, 20 December 1944, forecast persistent fog, with heavy snow showers expected on the high ground. It would remain cloudy, overcast and with a mild northeasterly wind. The temperatures were expected to fall below -15°C (5°F).

Artillery units within the Bastogne perimeter received coordinates from the outposts and elevated their guns to prevent the attacking Germans from entering the town. 'We were north of Metz when the Bulge began, in the small town of Launstraff, France, right on the German border, when we were ordered up to Bastogne, Belgium. We heard about the Bulge because we always tuned our half-track radios to the BBC. They overlapped, and around 02:00 we got a warning order from Division Headquarters saying they were getting ready to go north. Then around 08:00 we got our orders to be part of Combat Command B and go to Bastogne. A few days after arriving we moved across Bastogne out to the west to a small town called Senonchamps. We could reach the whole perimeter from there. It was a good location,' said Major Willis 'Crit' D. Crittenberger, HQ Battery, 420th Armored Field Battalion. 'The Germans trying to get by the armor and the airborne on the east side of town, they started to come around and they tried to come in the back door and that was where we were.'

General Hasso von Manteuffel, Commanding Officer, 5th Panzer Army, later recalled: 'It's surprising to me that Bastogne has an honourable place in American military history and Sankt Vith is hardly mentioned! The Battle of the Bulge was not fought solely at Bastogne.'

By 20 December in the central sector the 5th Panzer Army attacks had achieved some nominal gains. The villages of Noville and Bizory were taken, but Team O'Hara, supported by elements of the 327th Glider Regiment, decisively repulsed an attack against Marvie. Meanwhile, sealing off Bastogne was becoming a persistent matter of concern to the Germans. Manteuffel refused to authorize sufficient additional forces to physically capture the town, preferring instead to circumnavigate Bastogne and focus on reaching the Meuse River. He thought that containment would be sufficient to keep his supply lines open and facilitate the drive west; actual seizure was never on his agenda.

20 December passed with some heavy artillery duels and reorganization of the battle lines as some of the German forces attempted to open a path that led directly into Bastogne. Later that day, using tanks and self-propelled guns, the Germans opened a barrage against 501st positions between Bizory and Mont to the east of Bastogne. The bombardment cut all the telephone wires connecting the battalions with the rear, but failed to dislodge the paratroopers.

It was generally assumed by the German command that Bastogne would soon be completely surrounded and that Oberst Kokott's 26th *Volksgrenadier* Division in the wake of the other Panzer divisions would be able to capture it.

'I was out on the edge, in a foxhole. In this case, the ground was frozen, but we were in a barn lot with all the faeces and cattle stuff that was coming out, so it was easier to dig a foxhole there,' said demolitionist Ralph K. Manley, 501st Parachute Infantry Regiment, 101st Airborne Division. 'You can imagine what I must have smelled like. We disabled some tanks that were coming through with the bazooka, but they got very close. Oftentimes you maybe had two in a foxhole, but in this case it was just one because the ground was so hard to dig, at least on the surface with the snow. Also, you didn't want to reveal your position because of the black dirt on top of the white snow, so you had to get snow and cover over the soil that you had dug out of the foxhole.'

At no given time during the fighting did the attacking German forces significantly outnumber the American defenders, and the 101st Airborne was never completely isolated because they maintained communication with VIII Corps for the duration. They were also aware that Patton's 3rd Army was on the move and striking north. The level of discipline in the 3rd Army must have been quite phenomenal. The logistical challenges of disengaging a whole army of around 350,000 from one front, turn 90 degrees and advance north would have presented a gargantuan task to any commander, but Patton managed to accomplish this in a matter of days. For all his braggadocio this was going to be his moment and he knew it.

After Team Hyduke (formerly Team Desobry) and the 1st Battalion 506th left Noville and ran the gauntlet to reach the perimeter of Bastogne, the Gestapo arrived in the village. Father Louis Delvaux, the village priest who had a reputation for being a stubborn but compassionate man, watched aghast as these apparently French-speaking Gestapo men rounded up some of the male inhabitants of Noville. It was later claimed that they came from the Alsace region. When they had finished interrogating the suspects, the Gestapo marched the men to the main road in groups of three. There they made them scoop mud and debris with their hands. The suspects were in fact being forced to dig their own graves. After enduring about 15 minutes of this humiliation, the Gestapo took the men back to the municipal building. Then they told six of the younger men to stand apart from the others and motioned for the village priest and the schoolteacher to join them.

The eight men were marched off with their hands behind their heads. The Gestapo claimed that the spire of the church was being used to transmit information to the Allies, but failed to provide any actual evidence to support this claim. They marched the men to a small clearing just off the main Bastogne road and ordered them to get on their knees. They all knelt, except Father Delvaux, who remained upright. Then a Gestapo officer coldly placed his Luger in the mouth of one of his victims and pulled the trigger. The victim dropped like a stone as a jet of blood and brain tissue flared out from behind his head. The officer then turned to Father Delvaux and motioned for him to leave the group. The priest began protesting. 'What in the name of God are you doing?' he yelled.

'Stop this madness immediately. You are not acting like men.'

The Gestapo officer motioned again for the priest to leave the group, but Father Delvaux remained static and looked to the other men. According to a local witness, the priest said, 'Don't show these cowards any fear, my children. We are all going to meet our maker now. Go to him with a clear heart and the blessing of his humble servant here on earth.' Then Father Delvaux boldly walked up to the Gestapo officer and looked him in the eye. 'Kill me then, if you must. I'm not afraid of you.' 'I don't care,' said the Gestapo officer belligerently. 'You're all traitorous scum to me. You have all collaborated with the US army and will pay the price.' Just then a villager stepped forward and offered to take the place of the priest. Father Delvaux shook his head and told the man to go home to his family. He immediately added in a whisper that the man should get away from the area as soon as possible. Delvaux got to his knees, looked around at his fellow victims and the German guards and said: 'Courage, my sons. God is waiting to receive your souls.' Then he closed his eyes and felt the barrel of the Luger press against the back of his head. That was the last thing he felt. The victims were Father Louis Delvaux (50); Auguste Lutgen (45); brothers François and Felix Deprez (30 and 35); Joseph Rosière (35); Romain Henkinet (42); Roger Beaujean (21); and Michel Stranen (39). The father of François and Felix Deprez was a witness to their execution. The back of his house faced the open ground where it occurred.

Back in Bastogne, Jack Prior had established the 20th AIB Aid Station at the former Sarma Superette, an abandoned small supermarket on the Route du Neafchateau. He desperately needed additional medical personnel to augment his meagre unit. He had about 100 men in his charge, including 30 seriously wounded soldiers on stretchers and practically no medical equipment or medicines. The only other medical officer was a dentist named Lee Naftulin, who recruited Belgian nurse Renée Lemaire who told Jack that there was at least one other nurse in Bastogne. When Jack Prior learned about Augusta Chiwy, he called on her at her father's home. She agreed to assist in the full knowledge that, if the Germans succeeded in capturing Bastogne, she would likely be executed for having aided the Americans.

'By the time that I arrived at the aid station, it smelled like the devil's own breath,' said Augusta. 'It was a disgusting place, an unsanitary hovel. Those who could walk waded ankle-deep in dirty bandages covered in blood, piss and shit. Bits of uniforms were thrown piled in heaps that littered the freezing cold flagstone floor. In some places, blood had collected in shallow pools, diluted by melted snow brought in on the boots of the wounded and their litter bearers. There was no electricity and no running water in Bastogne. Those on the stretchers still wore remnants of uniforms that were stiff with dried blood and gore. The candles didn't help much. They just gave a miserable yellow glow. I remember the stinking haze caused by condensation from open wounds and desperate breathing. Some soldiers were shaking badly. When I close my eyes I can still smell the place.'

On 21 December, an American recon patrol went out to scout the German positions. They met a group of 101st paratroopers and proceeded down the road 2.5 km (1.5 miles) south-west of Bastogne until they discovered a sizeable force there that induced the patrol to perform a rapid about-turn. On that same day Bayerlein's Panzer Lehr launched an attack against the tiny village of Morhet. The 26th *Volksgrenadiers* captured Sibret, before moving west alongside a depleted 2nd Panzer Division. The increasing number of enemy forces bearing down on Bastogne prompted a reorganization of the American defensive perimeter, but despite a few setbacks they were doing as instructed and 'holding Bastogne'.

'December 21 was my birthday. I am no longer a teenager. That morning a German half-inch gun from in the nearby woods opened up point-blank on our vehicle. Most of the shots whizzed over us, a couple hit the ground in front of us. We were scared as hell,' wrote Albert Honowitz. 'We knew the Germans were in the woods and almost on top of us. We mounted the guns. They stopped firing. We weren't sure exactly where the Kraut gun that had fired at us was because the morning fog had camouflaged the woods. We opened up with our 1.5 in gun and two .50 cal. machine-guns at a spot we though the Kraut gun was.

'One half hour passed, nothing happened. Then the Kraut gun opened up on us again. We thought that there was no point of use staying in this position, [to] be shot at without being able to locate the firing position of the attacker. We let the artillery captain who had put us in that position know how we felt about it. The captain moved us to the next field to a position next to a large cluster of trees. There we dug 2 holes to protect ourselves, a hole large enough for 4 to sleep in and a hole large enough for 3 to sleep in. In that field were M-7 Priests letting the Germans have it with their 105 howitzers. Soon we decided to unhitch our trailer from the vehicle itself. As we unhitched the trailer we saw

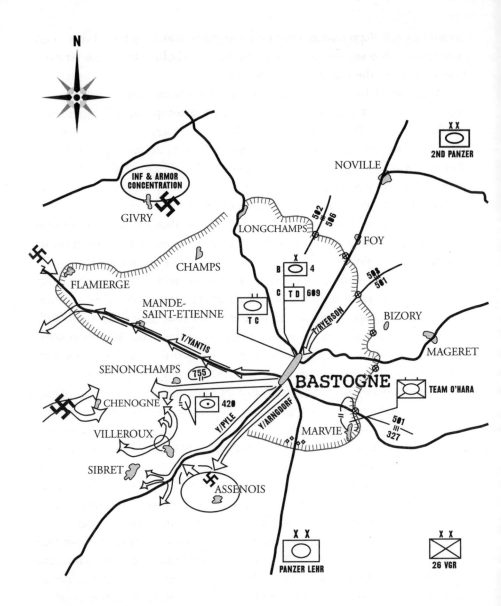

N

2ND PANZER

NOVILLE

INF & ARMOR
CONCENTRATION

GIVRY

LONGCHAMPS

502
506

FOY

CHAMPS

502
501

FLAMIERGE

MANDE-
SAINT-ETIENNE

B | 4

C | TD | 609

T/RYERSON

BIZORY

T/YANTIS

TC

MAGERET

SENONCHAMPS

755

BASTOGNE

TEAM O'HARA

CHENOGNE

420

Y/PYLE

Y/ARNGDORF

MARVIE

501
III
327

VILLEROUX

SIBRET

ASSENOIS

PANZER LEHR

26 VGR

SITUATION
BASTOGNE, BELGIUM
21 December 1944

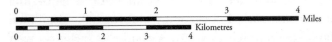

in the sky US P-47 Thunderbolts. The weather was very bad and we had not expected to see our buddies – the Thunderbolts. They were strafing the Krauts on the other side of the woods.

'We noticed that in among the cluster of trees were three tank destroyers - one just about 5 ft from our position. Clark, Thompson, and I went over to the TD [Tank Destroyer] closest to us to get a closer view of what was going there. We had heard their captain exclaiming to them that a German column was coming up behind the woods. (The woods from whence the German 20 mm gun had been firing at us.) The captain then pointed to the fogged-up woods and exclaimed that he could make out human figures moving about in front. He exclaimed that he thought that the figures moving about were German infantry coming up ready to close in on us with the protection of the German column in back of the woods.

'The captain ordered the Tank Destroyer, which was next to our position to open up with his .50 cal. MG [machine gun] and he ordered another TD to open up with his .50 cal. machine gun also. They both fired for about half a minute at the figures in the dark. All of a sudden the TD we were standing beside was hit with about 15 rounds of ammunition, ripping holes in the front of the tank and water and empty gas cans. We were all stunned but no one was hurt. Who had been firing at us? We soon found out: the other TD firing his .50 cal. MG. The smoke coming off the end of his machine gun barrel had blocked his vision. He had moved his machine gun carriage a little too much to the left and had hit his buddy's tank.

'Just after this unfortunate incident occurred, a major came running up to the captain who had given the order for the TDs to fire. He shouted, "You've been firing at our own men in front of the woods." They're our AA boys who were assigned to spray the woods. We found out later that it was Cpl. Capp's half-track they had fired at. Only one of his crew had been hit – the driver – Forrester. The AA half-track had been completely destroyed. Forrester's leg had been so badly mauled that it had to be amputated later on. The TD boys had made two serious errors that day. They had fired at our AA boys and at the same time had fired at each other's tank.

'Across the way from us in another field was Sgt. Vasseur's track. The night before Black, his cannoneer, had killed an infiltrating German coming up on them in the dark. Black got a pistol from the dead man. They threw his body in the ditch close by. A couple of our guys went over to see the dead Kraut. By the dead man's insignia, we saw he had been an officer. He was about 6 ft 3 in tall. After much snooping around we came back to our position. German 88s began landing in our field. Then things quieted down for a couple hours.

'During those couple of hours a battery of 155 howitzer men moved into the field of our previous position. We decided to do some more snooping around. A few of us took a walk over to the 155 men. We saw that they were in a terrific hurry setting up their heavy guns. They told us that the Germans with their mortars and 88s had driven them from a town a few miles away. "It was hell there," they said. Many of their own men were killed at that place. They soon set up, fired a couple of rounds, hitched their trailers back on and took off. It all happened in a matter of about 15 minutes. We couldn't understand why they had been given march orders so soon. They didn't know themselves. Apparently, the German lines were moving so fast that it was a useless task for the 155 howitzer boys.

'Just as the 155 boys left a bunch of German prisoners who had just been captured came trudging up the road. Many had on GI leggings, GI field jackets (one German wore a field jacket with the 10th Armd. Insignia on it), and many wore American combat boots. There was no doubt in our minds that they had murdered American prisoners, taken their clothes and shoes. There was no other way they could have gotten the American clothes and shoes. The GIs had become so enraged at the Germans with the American equipment that some of the Germans were forced to take their overcoats, jackets, shirts and undershirts off and walk in the bitter cold bare-chested.

'We soon went back to our position. 88s, mortars began landing in our field at a terrific rate. They began landing closer and closer to our position. Every time a shell came over we jumped in our holes. We knew the artillery men in our field were getting hit. We were pretty damn scared. Then 2 shells, one right back the other landed about 10 ft away, shrapnel whizzed above us. No one was hurt. We pressed the bottoms of our holes and shivered from fright. Then the shelling stopped. When we had been put in this position, the artillery captain whom we had been taking orders from, had told us to stay put and not move out of position unless he gave the order. The captain wasn't around. It was up to us to save our own lives.'

CHAPTER FOURTEEN

More of them than us

TO UNDERSTAND THE BATTLE OF the Bulge it's vitally important to understand the sheer magnitude of the area where it occurred. The different terrain in these regions was also affected, or rather afflicted, by different weather. Winter in the Ardennes meant that it would be freezing cold everywhere, but it could be foggy on the northern shoulder with clear skies in the south and vice versa. The high ground in the centre could be hit by buffeting Siberian winds while the river valleys were barely affected. While dense fog had impeded the fighting around Bastogne, some P-47 American fighters had used relatively clear skies to strafe Peiper's 19 km-long (12 mile) column in the Amblève valley as early as 18 December. In the long run, Allied air superiority would prove as constant a detriment to all the German forces engaged in the Ardennes as it did in the Normandy campaign.

American forces along the whole line were overtly aware that help was on the way, and this in turn inspired both collective and individual heroic actions that had but one purpose: to buy time. Owing to the closer proximity of American 1st Army units in the north, these troops

Prisoners captured during the Battle of the Bulge were transported to the Stalag IV-B prisoner-of-war camp near Mühlberg in Germany.

were inevitably going to arrive on the scene sooner than the 3rd Army heading up from France in the south. The strength and determination of the SS in the north would also provide a harder fight than the *Volksgrenadier* regiments in the central and southern sectors.

It's fair to deduce that the Battle of the Bulge was in fact a compendium of engagements fought under different circumstances against adversaries of varying ability equipped with different armour.

By 20 December it had become increasingly apparent to General Manteuffel that his 5th Panzer Army were falling behind schedule and taking Sankt Vith was now an imperative. Manteuffel would later say that the combined German Panzer armies lost the initiative as early as 18 December. On 19 December 6,800 GIs constituting two of the three 106th Infantry Division regiments had been captured, but there was still plenty of fight in the remaining 424th Regiment and their story was far from over. The same applied to the 106th Division's 589th Field Artillery who headed west and prepared to make a heroic stand in the face of overwhelming opposition. The terrible loss to the 106th was not the tragedy so frequently described in other accounts on the subject. The two regiments that were taken POW had mounted a staunch and concerted defence that had severely disrupted the Nazi timetable, and timing was everything to the Nazis. The whole premise of the battle depended on buying time and that's precisely what the 106th did even though, as one 106th GI plainly said, 'We got captured because there were more of them than us.'

Clifford B. Doxsee, HQ 3rd Battalion, 423rd Regiment, 106th Infantry Division, said, 'I was taken prisoner in the Battle of the Bulge, December 19, 1944 outside Schönberg, Belgium. The evening our train brought us from Limburg to Muhlberg, our captors first put us all through a "delousing" station. We were forced to remove all our clothes, go into a shower room naked and be thoroughly showered with hot water, which felt wonderful. Our clothes were sent through a chemical delousing treatment room while we were showering, so they came back purified if not washed. But before we could put our clothes back on, we had to endure inoculations, probably a good idea in principle, but one that hurt at the time because the needles were put into our chests rather than in arms or elsewhere. After receiving the inoculations and then dressing, we were taken to piles of overcoats and each given one. I received the coat originally used by a Belgian soldier, unbeautiful but wearable and much appreciated.

'At the Muhlberg camp there were prisoners of many nationalities, including Russians. Each group was housed separately in different compounds within the larger camp. But somehow it was possible for the differing groups to move back and forth during daylight, and we saw Russians come many times into the British non-commissioned officers' compound where we were housed temporarily, seeking food. Russia had never signed the Geneva Convention on treatment of prisoners in wartime, and since the Russian government mistreated Germans held in the USSR, the Germans felt quite able to reciprocate. Hence, these Russians were literally starving, and to fend off death as long as possible they wandered into the compounds of other nationalities to scrounge the garbage and leftovers that Allied prisoners would not eat. We remained at the large prison camp near Muhlberg, Germany, for about 14 days until sent off to Dresden.'

The failure or success of the Nazi offensive also depended on gaining control of vital road networks like the ones that converged on Sankt Vith. This would have to coincide with the elimination of the American-occupied salient that had become known as the 'Fortified Goose Egg'. Repeated attempts by the 62nd *Volksgrenadier* Division to break through the breach that existed between Combat Command B, 9th Armored Division and the 424th Infantry Regiment on 21 December were stoically resisted. By the end of the day the 7th Armored Division had seen little action on the northern flank, the northern perimeter of the Goose Egg, due to concentrated enemy efforts to penetrate the southern flank that hadn't achieved the desired results. At the same time the 28th Division's 112th Infantry Regiment had succeeded in consolidating the line and linking up with the 424th, the only regiment of the 106th Infantry Division to avoid capture and survive relatively intact. The 106th commander General Alan Jones later suffered a massive heart attack induced by the incredible pressure that he had been forced to sustain during those opening days of the Battle of the Bulge. His son was with one of the regiments captured out on the Schnee Eifel, along with Buffalo Bill's grandson and notable American writer Kurt Vonnegut.

On the northern shoulder, *Kampfgruppe Peiper* had been compelled to return to the village of La Gleize and attempted to head west to Stoumont unaware that they would face some serious opposition. Their supply route that went through Stavelot had been severed on 19 December and now there was in effect no way back. Peiper was vulnerable and exposed as his column ascended the high ground in the direction of Targnon, west of La Gleize. He would have had a panoramic view of the Amblève valley, but beyond Targnon the road dips into another steep valley and that was where danger lurked.

The 30th Division's 119th Regiment travelled in two columns south to Remouchamps at the eastern rim of the Amblève valley. At this juncture they separated and sent one detachment comprised of the 2nd Battalion and the cannon company to Werbomont, where the 82nd Airborne had arrived, while the second, better-equipped, column navigated the road that descends into the Amblève valley. The 2nd Battalion reached Lienne Creek after dark and quickly established ad hoc defences on the hills roughly 4.8 km (3 miles) east of Werbomont, at the place where Peiper had watched the bridge being blown by engineers.

The 119th's 3rd Battalion leading column reached Stoumont after dark and set up a perimeter defence. Recon patrols were dispatched and had little difficulty discovering the location of the enemy, whose pickets were smoking and talking less than a mile away. Around 40 German vehicles were reported bivouacked east of Stoumont. The remainder of the American force assembled some 4 km (2.5 miles) north-west of Stoumont, while the 400th Armored Field Artillery Battalion that had been requisitioned during the march south moved its batteries forward under cover of darkness. The following day they would go head-to-head with the SS, but they didn't call the 30th Infantry Division 'Roosevelt's SS' for nothing.

By the time Peiper reached Stoumont his unit was still relatively well equipped. It comprised a mixed battalion of Mark IV tanks and Panthers from the 1st SS Panzer Regiment, a battalion of armoured infantry from the 2nd SS Panzer Grenadier Regiment, a flak battalion, a battalion of Tiger tanks that had joined Peiper at Stavelot, a battery of 105 mm (4 in) self-propelled guns, and a tough company of paratroopers from the 3rd Parachute Division that had hitched a ride on Peiper's tanks and accompanied him into the valley from Honsfeld. *Kampfgruppe Peiper* had incurred some losses while attempting to hammer a path to the Meuse, but their most critical consideration was fuel, which was running desperately low.

Earlier in the battle Peiper had chosen to circumnavigate Malmedy entirely in favour of an alternative route to the Meuse River. After the apparently abject failure of 'Operation Greif', Otto Skorzeny's 150 Panzer Brigade had arrived on the heights to the south-west of the town that has roads converging on the Avenue du Pont du Warche, the main western route out of Malmedy.

Out in Malmedy a squad of GIs from 30th Division's 120th Infantry Regiment had been given the task of guarding the bridge on the Avenue du Pont du Warche at the westerly approach to the town. They had been personally reassured that there was no German armour in the vicinity and there was nothing to fear. Pfc Francis S. Currey, a 19-year-old BAR gunner, single-handedly disabled three German tanks, one of which was painted olive drab and had fake US insignia on the turret and flanks. He also destroyed two half-tracks, killed several German soldiers, and in the process rescued five of his comrades from certain death or imprisonment. For his incredibly brave actions Francis Currey was awarded the Congressional Medal of Honor along with the Belgian equivalent, the Belgian Military Order of Leopold II with Palm. Eisenhower later said, 'If the Germans had taken the bridge at Malmedy and the US Army Depot at Liege, the war would have been six weeks longer. So actually, I personally approved the citation.'

'You should have seen the fucking headquarters people who came down to see the situation!' said Francis Currey. 'The first tank we took out had turned sideways so that the gun was facing toward Malmedy and his back was toward us. The tank was at an angle but he had the turret turned to cover the city. I had a good shot at it. He was blind and didn't see us at all. You had to get within 50 ft because that was the range of the bazooka. Lucero loaded the bazooka. I fired and hit it where the turret turns on the chassis. It went right in there. Of course, it really screwed it up and they got the hell out of there. I later found out the tank crashed into a building because he was in such a hurry to get out of there!

'There were three tanks in front of me, one in the middle and the others on the sides. The anti-tank gun had been demolished. I wanted to get a better look. There was a little hedge so I crawled down and saw guys trapped in foxholes down there. One of them was a sergeant and he was closest to the gun. I said, "They haven't seen me yet, that hedge is blocking me. This is what I am going to do. Is that your half-track down there?" He said, "Yes." I then asked, "Do you have anti-tank grenades?" He replied, "Yes, I have a couple boxes of them."

I then told him, "I'm going to go back and bring them up. How about a launcher?" He said, "Yes, I'll tell you where to find one, you have to have an M1 to use it." I said, "You guys just sit tight!" There was a lull, no fighting was going on. It was a stalemate. I went back to the half-track and got a box of grenades and the other stuff. They still hadn't seen me. The AT [anti-tank] sergeant then said, "We've got one guy who is pretty well shot up." I said, "I'm going to fire these grenades." This was part of my training. I was taught at Benning that an anti-tank grenade would not take out a tank. But when it hits the tank it will make a hell of a big flame, a lot of smoke, and a lot of noise.

'The tanks were not spread out. So I started to fire these grenades, a few here, a couple there. I used them up. The tankers abandoned the tanks; they must have thought a big AT gun was firing. I then set up a .30-caliber machine gun. It had been used to back up the AT gun. I then sprayed the area with machine-gun fire. I told the trapped AT crew to get out one by one, but to make sure that someone was with the wounded man. I was the last one out with the sergeant.'

It was individual actions such as those of Francis Currey that repeatedly confounded and frustrated German attempts to remain on schedule. Currey assumed command and dealt with the situation accordingly, but there were many such instances during the Battle of the Bulge.

When John Schaffner and the remaining three 105 mm howitzers of his 589th Field Artillery Battalion, formerly attached to the 106th, arrived at a crossroad junction at a place called Baraque de Fraiture their commander Major Arthur C. Parker told the unit to dig in. This was one of the highest, most frighteningly-exposed locations in the Ardennes central region, and the only place that has ski slopes. But it was no ski resort for these young GIs who had endured the full fury of the initial onslaught and there could have been no more terrifying prospect than the one facing them when they dug in at Baraque de Fraiture. Dense mist obscured their depth of vision, and the smallest noise resonated through the all-encapsulating gloom as they waited and waited. Temperatures dipped to well below zero and the men did everything they could to stave off the numbing cold. They knew that the Germans were heading their way because there had already been a few exchanges, but that's about all they knew. GIs huddled together in foxholes, checked their rifles and machine guns and kept their heads down. The long and bitter nights on that exposed plateau in the Ardennes in the winter of

1944 greatly demoralized many GIs. Teeth chattered and fingers froze as tense moments passed in anticipation of the approaching storm. To some extent the pervasive cold subdued the fear and the longing for warmth eliminated almost all other considerations. During the night an 80-man patrol from the 560th *Volksgrenadier* Division and the 2nd SS Panzer Division began probing and initiating sporadic attacks against the American-held position at Baraque de Fraiture. The 2nd SS Panzer Division (*Das Reich* or 'The Empire') had a fearsome reputation. Some of its units had perpetrated the horrendous massacre of innocents at the French village of Oradour sur Glane. There were many tough, embittered veterans among their ranks who had experienced years of hard combat in both the east and the west.

'So, here we sat in this hole in the ground, just waiting and watching, until about midnight, when we could hear strange noises in the fog. It was very dark and our visibility was extremely limited, but we were able to discern what was making the strange noise, as about a dozen German soldiers riding on bicycles came into view. They stopped in the road when they came on the mines,' John Schaffner acerbically quipped. 'We were joined by some people of the 203rd AAA, 7th Armored Division, equipped with three M-16 half-tracks mounted with a brace of four .50-caliber machine guns and an M8 Scout Car with a 37 mm cannon. I thought at the time I'd hate to be in front of that quad-50 when it went off. Little did I know at the time that I would be.'

John Schaffner was a forward artillery observer who knew that the Germans could strike at any minute and also knew that, when that occurred, along with his comrades he could be blown to pieces or maimed beyond recognition. What he experienced at those crossroads between 19–23 December was one of the most intense and bitter engagements of the whole battle. Major Parker was wounded during the first hours but his unit continued to help fend off the 2nd SS. Finally, after almost four days of fighting, what remained of the defenders of Baraque de Fraiture abandoned this key position. But their indomitable tenacity against these terrifying adversaries again won valuable time for the American forces.

'At about 15:30 in the afternoon all hell broke loose. Half of my crew were in the house getting warm. I made a run for it to get my men back to the gun to be ready for the assault,' said John Gatens, Battery A, 589th Field Artillery Battalion. 'Once inside, I got my men together, but we never did make it back to the gun. I was standing in the doorway ready to go when a shell hit. The concussion picked me up and sent me flying against the back wall. I sat there a few minutes in a daze. I had to feel for my legs and arms to make sure they were still there.

'The shelling stopped and at the same time there was a German tank outside the door. His gun was pointing in the door. A German officer shouted out, "Are you coming out or do I tell this guy to fire?" No one can be a hero when a tank is staring down your throat. Some of the surrounding area men had already been rounded up and were standing in rows on the road. We filed out of the building and joined the rows of men. They made us remove our overcoats so they could search us. They took anything of value. I was wearing my wife's (although not at that time) high school ring. That was gone. The other items were money, cigarettes and chocolate (every GI had a few concentrated chocolate bars called D bars that didn't melt. They were hard and you had to scrape off shreds, or if you had good teeth you could break off a chunk), my gloves, my wool knit cap and my fountain pen. For some reason they would not take wedding rings. Either they were superstitious or they had some respectability. It was now approximately 17:50 hours. The weather was bitter cold, but now I had no overcoat, gloves or wool knit cap. It was a cold helmet and field jacket from here on. How I made that winter with just those clothes I'll never know.' John Gatens spent the rest of the war in captivity. The stone barn where he was captured is still there. The location was renamed 'Parker's Crossroads'. 82nd Airborne commander General Gavin later wrote a letter to Major Parker about his heroic stand:

Dear Major Parker

In the Battle of the Bulge, I was commanding the 82nd Airborne Division and we were originally given the front from Trois-Ponts to Vielsalm, including Thier Dumont. We got into very heavy fighting when the 1st Regiment of the 1st SS Panzer Division broke through the Engineers' front and occupied Stoumont. We then had the remainder of the Division at Trois-Ponts. At the same time, in twenty-four hours it came clear that the Germans were bypassing us, moving to the west [and] turning north when the opportunity presented itself. The 7th Armored and part of the 28th Infantry Division and a few of the 106th came through our lines. I was in the town of Fraiture the afternoon when you made your great stand at the crossroads. I had sent a Company from the 325th under Capt. Woodruff, to the crossroads to help hold it, so I started over in that direction myself. The fire was so intense, however, that there was no way of getting there without crawling through the woods, and it was a distance away. I decided that I had better get some more help, so I sent to the extreme left flank of the division for the 2nd Battalion of the 504th, where it had the 1st SS Regiment of the 1st Panzer Division bottled. In doing so, we uncovered the Germans and during the night of Christmas Eve they slipped through the 505th Parachute Infantry. Nevertheless, I got the 2nd Battalion of the 504th to back up the crossroads come what may. The stand that your defenders made at the crossroads was one of the great actions of the war. It gave us at least twenty-four hours' respite so I thank you for that, and all the brave soldiers who were under your command.

With best regards
James A. Gavin
Lieutenant General (retired)

SS-Obersturmführer Horst Gresiak, commander of the II Battalion, Second SS Panzer Regiment, the unit which eventually overran the American defences at Baraque de Fraiture said, 'Although brief, it was the most violent and the toughest battle that I experienced during the entire war.'

Down on the southern shoulder in Luxembourg, the 4th Infantry Division was seizing the initiative. General 'Tubby' Barton felt confident enough to launch a counter-attack. He said, 'The best way to handle these Heinies is to fight 'em.' The American counter-attack was initiated on 22 December and initially each side jockeyed for position, but it was becoming increasingly apparent to all that the German effort to charge through Luxembourg was beginning to dissipate. The 4th Infantry Division, supported by the 10th Armored Division Combat Command, managed to hold and contain the southern shoulder of the German penetration, just like the 99th Infantry and 7th Armored Divisions had held the northern shoulder.

Down in Bastogne, Albert Honowitz, B Battery, 796th Anti-aircraft Artillery Automatic Weapons Battalion, 3rd Army, wrote: 'At 2:00 in the morning an officer came over to us. We had all fallen asleep in the cold night. Blackie Zaparo was supposed to have been on guard at the time, he had also fallen asleep. Blackie soon got up when he heard the officer talking. The officer gave him instructions to move the track up to the corner of the field as he considered it for some reason or another a better spot for us. Blackie was also told to awaken everyone at 6:00 in the morning so everyone could be on the alert. Blackie moved the track to the corner of the field. When daylight arrived shelling of our field began but it wasn't very heavy.

'We ate hot chow that bitter cold morning with the 420th [Field Artillery, A Battery]. They had been with us since we came to Bastogne. It was our first hot meal in three days. We had hot pancakes, rolled oats cereal, hot coffee. I went up for second servings. I'll never forget that hot meal. It really hit the spot. We had been eating cold C and K rations in the very cold weather. Being that Senonchamps was just across the way, Thompson decided to take a walk into town to let Lt. Palmaccio know about the trouble we had been having with the motor. We went into town after Palmaccio said that it was OK that we do that. While we waited for our track to be repaired we stayed at the Battery, 1st and 2nd platoon CP, which was all in one building. We found about half the battery's men there, as most of them were in for track repairs also.

'There were three pretty Belgian girls who lived in that house which had been converted into a CP. The three girls had refused to leave their house to be evacuated. I never found out whether they were sisters or from different families. But I know that they were the only civilians left in the tiny yet undamaged town. The three girls heated up water for the boys to wash and water for coffee. They seemed very happy to do whatever they could for us. The girls didn't seem the least worried that the town was in danger of imminent capture and that the German horde entering the town would, on finding the three girls, with evidences that they were aiding the Americans, rape them. Three innocent girls in the midst of accusation as that stand little chance of not being raped, murdered, or both.

'In this CP house was our first chance since we left the suburbs of Bastogne to get under a roof with four walled rooms. For some reason or another we felt very safe in this house, although the town was being shelled. By looking at the faces of the men in this CP house it could be plainly seen that the men had had the daylights scared from them for hour after hour. None of the men had the slightest evidence of a smile on their faces. Soon Lt. Palmaccio came in and told us that the Germans were only about 7 miles from Senonchamps [and] that a German general had given us an ultimatum to surrender by 11:00 that nite or else be "eliminated." We also heard that the commander of the 101st replied, "Nuts."

'Lt. Palmaccio let it be known that "as American soldiers we will never surrender" and "we'll fight for this town, from house to house, and room to room." This remark made us half laugh and at the same time made us very solemn. Another remark he made put us in the same feeling: "They'll be reading about the defence we put up here in history class." Soon Cpl. Marsh came in and told us how Katz, his gunner, was killed the nite before. Shrapnel had landed right in the hole that Katz and Gehebe were in. A big chunk hit Kats in the temple and killed him instantly. Gehebe was very badly wounded in the arm and leg. Katz was the first man from B Battery to be killed. B Battery already had many wounded. Katz and I had gone to see a pretty girl together the night we stayed in Luxembourg City. The news of the death greatly shocked me.

'Some of the fellas in the CP seemed on the verge of battle fatigue. Black from Sgt. Vasseur's track and Topper from Sgt. Meadows' track had become so shocked from the happenings that they were crying. In the CP house we could now hear the Krauts shelling the road into Senonchamps. The barrage on the road was so terrific that the town of Senonchamps was like being cut off from Bastogne. The barrage became so bad that the repaired tracks in Senonchamps couldn't get back into the fields. Hoyt Ross's track, trying to leave Senonchamps was hit and had to come back into town.

'I had been waiting all this time for the other fellas to wash and was about to wash myself for the first time in three days, when Lt. Palmaccio came up to me and said, "Honowitz, put your shirt on." That's all he said. He motioned for me to come outside with him. I did as he told me. He pointed to the road, which to everyone seemed like suicide to go through. He told me that Topper had refused to go with his crew through that road out into the field which was being shelled almost as bad as the road. Topper was crying and Palmaccio wasn't going to force him to go. "Two AA tracks needed in that field," Palmaccio said, and I was to take Topper's place on Sgt. Meadows' crew.

'I left all my personal belongings on Thompson's trailer, took only my bedroll with me, hopped up on Meadows' track which was already in the street. Their crew had been waiting there for someone to take Topper's place. Soon, Capt. Walker, our Battalion Commander came to us and gave us a pep talk which really made us feel worse than better. He said, "it would be in the field, but someone's got to go and your crew and Cpl. Evanich's happened to be the ones. Your crew would go first, then in about 10 minutes Evanich's would follow."

'Palmaccio gave Meadows' driver, Lenzo, instructions to follow him up the road and that he'd go into the field to show us where he wanted us to set up in position. The road was still being shelled. Luckily for us not a shell dropped on the road or in the field at the time. Our position was about 15ft from a wooden pigpen and about 10ft from a little brick house. There were freshly-made shell holes in this field, it seemed even more than in the other fields we had been in. Palmaccio told us to "dig, dig, dig." We dug separate holes. Some were already half dug when we got there. The top layer of frozen snow and earth was hard breaking through with our shovels but the ground was easy going underneath.

'It began to get dark. Our field was being shelled but it wasn't as bad as it had been before we got there. A few 88s landed close by us, sky-bursts began landing in our field later on in the evening. Many artillery boys were wounded.

'From the previous day's shell our field was littered with M-7 Priests whom had had direct hits. One M-7 Priest artillery vehicle burned all nite and lit up about one quarter of the field. When it became total dark the Krauts resumed shelling the road into Senonchamps. They barraged the road all night long. Because of the sky-bursts I put three rows of logs over the top of my dugout, with dirt over the logs and then snow for camouflage. I continually worked on my dugout until about 12:00

that night, when I went to sleep in the hog pen, where we had decided to sleep for the night. The bodies of pigs at least kept the place warm. We didn't mind their odour at all.'

CHAPTER FIFTEEN

It isn't over yet

BASTOGNE WAS SURROUNDED, A CITY under siege, but this fact hadn't diluted or detracted from the fighting spirit of its American defenders. On the perimeter, in foxholes and slit trenches, GIs shivered and drew up the blankets together in a vain attempt to stave off the encumbering cold. The area was still shrouded in dense fog, and exacerbating an already bad situation over a foot of snow had accumulated over the previous few days. Some artillery units were reporting that they were down to their last shell, as all stocks of ammunition became seriously depleted. Resupply was now a matter of great urgency to all concerned. First those clouds had to clear.

There are a number of published accounts regarding the surrender ultimatum that was delivered to General McAuliffe during those dark December days, some of which are incredibly detailed, while others are less accurate. What precisely transpired that day may never be known, but here is one version of the events.

It was around 11:30, 22 December, when four Germans, two officers and two senior enlisted men, emerged out of the fog on the Arlon Road from the direction of Remoifosse, just south of Bastogne. The senior officer was Major Wagner of General von Lüttwitz's 47th Panzer Corps. The junior officer was Lt. Hellmuth Henke from the Panzer Lehr Operations Section. Carrying a couple of white flags, they tentatively approached the lines of the 327th Glider Infantry Regiment. One of the officers was carrying a briefcase under his arm. They walked past the foxhole of a bazooka team in front of the Kessler farm and stopped at Pfc Leo Palma's foxhole. Lieutenant Henke spoke English: 'I want to see the commanding officer of this section.' Palma was dumbfounded, but Staff Sergeant Carl E. Dickinson, who was manning a position in close proximity, walked out to the road and beckoned the group to approach him, whereupon the Germans explained that they had a written message for the American commander in Bastogne.

The German officers agreed to wear blindfolds before being escorted to the next location. At this point, Pfc First Class Ernest D. Premetz, a medic from the 327th Medical Detachment, joined them. Premetz had a working knowledge of German, which proved superfluous at that moment because the German captain had a good command of the English language. What ensued was a protracted game of 'pass the parcel' as the Germans were taken inside the Kessler farm and presented to Lt. Leslie Smith. Smith blindfolded the two officers and, leaving the two enlisted men under guard, they took a circuitous route to 327th's F Company CP, which was a large foxhole located in a wooded area about a quarter of a mile away. Shortly after arriving at the command post, they were joined by Capt. James F. Adams, the F Company Commander, who had been at a forward observation post when he was notified of the arrival of the Germans.

The F Company Executive Officer, Lt. William J. Herzke, relayed the message by phone to their Battalion Command Post in Marvie. The 2nd Battalion Command Post then notified the 327th Regimental Headquarters in Bastogne. Major Alvin Jones received the call because Regimental Commander Colonel Bud Harper was preoccupied with the inspection of his unit's positions. Jones notified the Division Headquarters in Bastogne. He was told to retrieve the message and bring it to the Division Headquarters. He drove to the F Company Command Post and was given the message. The two blindfolded officers were detained in the woods adjacent to the foxhole Command Post.

Jones went to the 101st HQ in Bastogne and presented the information to General McAuliffe's acting Chief of Staff, Lieutenant Colonel Ned D. Moore, who immediately went to Brigadier General Anthony C. McAuliffe's quarters adjacent to the communications centre in the basement of the Heintz army barracks. One version of the events claims that when the information was relayed McAuliffe was asleep and uttered the word 'Nuts!' while he was getting out of his sleeping bag. Considering the time of day the message was delivered, this it is highly unlikely. It's more probable that he was sitting at his desk. McAuliffe's initial response to the ultimatum was, 'They want to surrender to us?', to which Moore replied, 'No sir. The Nazis are demanding we surrender to them.' McAuliffe guffawed when he heard this.

According to G-3 Lt. Col. Harry Kinnard and others present, when McAuliffe received the German message he was very much awake. He read it, crumpled it into a ball, threw it in a wastepaper basket, and muttered, 'Aw, nuts! We are not surrendering, gentlemen. Now, the question is, how do we articulate that to the German commander?' The room went quiet. The officers in McAuliffe's command post attempted to draft an official reply when, according to witnesses and Kinnard's own version of events, he interceded: 'That first remark of yours would be hard to beat.'

General McAuliffe didn't immediately grasp what the G-3 man was implying so Kinnard reminded him: 'You said what you always say in these situations: "Nuts!"' This prompted a spontaneous round of applause from everyone present. Encouraged by the enthusiastic response, McAuliffe decided to send that one-word message back to the Germans and made history.

Harper returned to the F Company Command Post. Henke asked if the reply was written or verbal. Harper answered it was written as he placed it in the hand of the still-blindfolded German Major. Henke inquired as to the nature of the reply, adding that, if it was affirmative, they were authorized to negotiate further. Harper said, 'The reply consists of a single word, "NUTS!"' Henke looked puzzled: 'Is that reply negative or affirmative?' 'The reply is decidedly not affirmative,' Harper replied, adding, 'If you continue this foolish attack, your losses will be tremendous.' Henke translated the information to Major Wagner, who nodded as he pensively digested what he was being told.

Then Harper drove the two blindfolded German officers back to the Kessler farm where they were rejoined by Pfc Premetz, among others. The

General Anthony Clement McAuliffe, acting commander of the US 101st Airborne Division troops defending Bastogne, made the most famous verbal riposte of World War II.

blindfolds were removed to allow the Germans to examine the reply. Henke raised his eyebrows and shrugged his shoulders as he asked, 'What does this mean?' Harper and Premetz discussed how to explain it. Harper suggested something to the effect of, 'Tell them to take a flying shit!' Premetz thought about it, then straightened up, faced the Germans and said, '*Du kannst zum Teufel gehen.*' He told Harper it meant, 'You can go to Hell.' Then Harper said, 'If you continue to attack, we will kill every goddamn German that tries to break into this city.' Henke replied, 'We will kill many Americans. This is war.' Harper then said, 'On your way Bud, and good luck to you.' Harper later regretted wishing them good luck. The Germans gave a military salute and began to walk away. They stopped momentarily as Harper cupped his hands to his mouth and shouted, 'If you don't know what I am talking about, simply go back to your commanding officer and tell him to just plain "Go to Hell". The German party returned to their lines. Captain Adams recorded the time as 14:00 hours.

The German officers later presented the 'NUTS' reply to Panzer Lehr commander General Bayerlein. Lüttwitz reminded Bayerlein that Bastogne was not his objective and ordered the Panzer Lehr Division to proceed around Bastogne to Rochefort and leave Bastogne to the 26th *Volksgrenadier* Division.

Although von Rundstedt thought the time was ripe to make a *coup de grace* against Bastogne, he didn't offer clear instructions to Manteuffel as to how this could be achieved. Manteuffel was busy hammering a route to the Meuse River and getting dangerously close to his objective. He passed the information to von Lüttwitz who felt that he wasn't yet ready to launch an all-out assault. This is why he arranged to send an ultimatum to General McAuliffe. It was a gamble that ultimately failed and Manteuffel had no prior knowledge of it.

Albert Honowitz wrote: 'December 23, 1944: I continually worked on my dugout while on guard in the early hours of the morning. Our field wasn't shelled too heavy that day but the dreaded sky-bursts kept us in and out of our holes all day long. One sky-burst landed in back of the little brick house. One 88 landed about 10 ft from me as I lay in my dugout, shrapnel knocked dirt into the opening. I was very scared. We threw all our German souvenirs away as we feared if we were captured the Germans would surely seek revenge after finding some of their own equipment on us.'

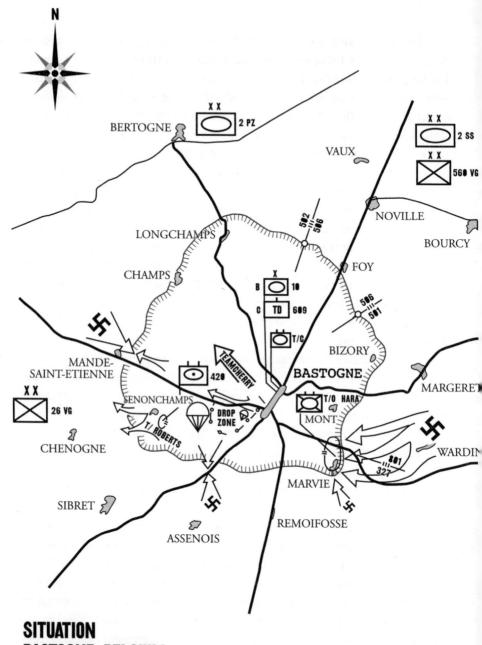

N

BERTOGNE

2 PZ

VAUX

2 SS

560 VG

NOVILLE

LONGCHAMPS

502
|||
506

FOY

BOURCY

CHAMPS

B **10**

C TD **609**

T/C

506
|||
501

BIZORY

BASTOGNE

MANDE-
SAINT-ETIENNE

420

TEAMCHERRY

MARGERET

26 VG

SENONCHAMPS

T/ ROBERTS

DROP
ZONE

T/O HARA

MONT

CHENOGNE

WARDIN

501
|||
327

SIBRET

MARVIE

ASSENOIS

REMOIFOSSE

SITUATION
BASTOGNE, BELGIUM
23 December 1944

0   1   2   3   4
Miles
Kilometres
0   1   2   3   4

The skies above Bastogne finally cleared on 23 December, and by mid-morning US Pathfinders had parachuted in from two C-47s to mark the landing zones (LZs) and drop zones (DZs). 'Operation Repulse' became one of the most accurate air resupply drops of World War II. Around midday, the soldiers and civilians gazed heavenward as the skies above Bastogne began to fill with squadrons of loaded C-47s roaring into view. During the afternoon, three 9th Air Force fighter groups provided tactical support, and by the close of the day 249 C-47s had provided the besieged city with 5,000 artillery shells, almost as many mortar rounds, 2,300 grenades, a dozen boxes of morphine, 300 units of plasma and 1,500 bandages. In total, 208 tonnes (230 tons) of badly needed supplies and rations were expertly delivered. While GIs swarmed around the DZs, rapaciously collecting everything that they could haul away, P-47s harried Manteuffel's Panzers, trucks, and assault guns with bullets, napalm and high explosives. Tracks in the fresh snow made them easy targets. A further 217 tonnes (240 tons) of supplies were dropped on the following day, Christmas Eve.

Despite the air resupply drops, German attacks increased in intensity. With a defensive perimeter of only 20 km (12.5 miles) in circumference, and more than 3,000 civilians still trapped in cellars inside, the German shelling reached every corner. At the 101st HQ over 600 wounded had been packed into the former shooting range. A couple of the medics sprinkled the sawdust floor with carbolic acid but this did little to relieve the stench of death and excrement. In the city itself the streets were practically deserted, save for the odd wraith-like inhabitant wandering like a lost soul between the ruins. Smouldering embers permeated the stale, damp air, mixing with the nauseous stench of decaying corpses; starving stray dogs and cats foraged frenetically among the piles of rubble that were once homes, shops and businesses. Bing Crosby's *White Christmas* crackled mockingly on a requisitioned gramophone. The decorations that had been put up in anticipation of the approaching festivities were scattered like discarded confetti around the shell holes and debris that punctuated the pavements and roads.

Dead bodies and limbs lay everywhere, some covered, some exposed, their frozen forms accentuated against the unremitting snow and cold. Smoke billowed from the ruins of now-unrecognizable structures. It was difficult to discern which buildings had been shops and which hadn't. Burned-out hulks of abandoned US army vehicles were scattered

Troops from the 101st Airborne watch as supplies are parachuted in during Operation Repulse.

intermittently along the entire street. Bastogne had become a derelict ghost town.

That evening, a squadron of Luftwaffe bombers was heading for Bastogne. The Junkers 88 S-3s had set off from Dedelstorf, just over the German border. 20th AIB surgeon Jack Prior was enjoying a glass of champagne with Augusta Chiwy in a small room next door to the aid station when a 227 kg (500 lb) bomb impacted. The shock wave blew Augusta clean through a kitchen wall. The other nurse, Renée Lemaire, who was inside the aid station, was tragically blown to pieces. Both Jack and Augusta survived.

On Christmas Day General McAuliffe received a welcome message from General Patton informing him that the 3rd Army was close by. The defenders and residents of Bastogne were oblivious to the fact that the Germans had been facing stiff resistance everywhere in the Ardennes and, although there would be further attempts to take the city, to the better informed it was becoming apparent that Hitler's last offensive in the west was doomed.

General Heinz Kokott launched a fresh offensive against Bastogne in the early hours of Christmas Day. There are a number of reasons why these attacks ultimately failed in their objectives. Bad planning and insufficient use of the road network around Bastogne had created calamitous traffic jams for the German vehicles that again severely disrupted their timetable. This was exacerbated by inclement weather conditions that had been favourable up until 23 December. After that time, a mild thaw in some areas had forced German armour to keep to the roads, further restricting their manoeuvrability.

The following day, 26 December, Patton arrived in Bastogne. Reminiscent of a battering ram, his 3rd Army had punched a corridor through German positions to the south and south-east of Bastogne. In some places the corridor was only a mile wide but that was enough to get the wounded out and get supplies in. Patton was heard to say to a sergeant of the 101st Airborne: 'It isn't over yet!'

CHAPTER SIXTEEN

Mops and pincers

THE MOST CONTROVERSIAL APPOINTMENT OF any commander during the Battle of the Bulge on the Allied side was that of Montgomery. No other commission extracted as much hate and derision from his subordinates. American authors have disseminated their disdain over the years and very few have defended the choice. Then there's the British batch that have staunchly defended Montgomery for purely nationalistic considerations. Nevertheless, the question remains. Was he the right man for the right job? 20 December was allocated by Eisenhower as the day to assume command of the northern components of the US 1st Army. Eisenhower had met with Patton and Bradley at Verdun on 19 December. The Supreme Allied Commander ordered Patton to make a sharp left turn with his 3rd Army and hit Rundstedt in the flanks from the south, a couple of days after Bradley had ordered Patton to temporarily suspend his Saar offensive and disengage and displace his 3rd to the north. All American forces north of the line Givet–Houffalize–Prum were transferred to Monty's command.

Two British generals, Jock Whiteley and Kenneth Strong, initially broached Bedell Smith on the subject. Neither were particularly

Christmas Day in Bastogne. Members of the 101st Airborne examine the damage done by the Luftwaffe bombers the day before.

fervent admirers of Montgomery, but the situation demanded an experienced commander. When Bedell Smith was informed of the proposed appointment, despite recovering from a serious bout of flu, he leapt out of his bed and flew into a seething rage. His deep hatred and insidious bias against Monty clouded all other considerations at that precise moment. But despite his vitriolic condemnation of the proposal he was compelled to acquiesce. Considering the escalating gravity of the situation there was no other feasible choice at that time. The simple root of the problem was 1st Army commander Courtney Hodges. His inherent inability to respond to the German attacks and ensuing inertia gave SHAEF little option. So it was Bedell Smith, arguably Monty's harshest critic and most vociferous detractor, who proposed the appointment to Eisenhower but the recommendation to put Monty in charge had to come from a senior American general.

The appointment was predictably met with wails of derision among the American generals, and almost every order that Monty issued from that point on was reluctantly complied with through gritted teeth. There's no doubt that the self-aggrandizing British field marshal was cautious, but his considerations were usually swayed by the need to avoid mass Allied casualties. This hadn't been the case at Operation Market Garden, but now Monty was determined to do battle on his terms and on the condition that he had a superior force in place that could accomplish the task, just as he had done at El Alamein. The danger was of course that he would be overly magnanimous in victory, if victory were achieved. Although satisfactory results were achieved thanks to Monty's judgement, what transpired after the battle was actually worse than anyone could have possibly imagined.

Meanwhile, in the northern sector US forces had made substantial preparations to close down *Kampfgruppe Peiper*. On 20 December, 3rd Armored Division's Combat Command B had organized three task forces to go immediately to the assistance of the 30th Division. The biggest and best equipped of these was Task Force Lovelady, led by Lieutenant Colonel William B. Lovelady. The other task forces were Task Force McGeorge (Major K. T. McGeorge) and Task Force Jordan (Captain John W. Jordan). Each task force had a distinct allocation. Task Force McGeorge was designated to attack La Gleize and pass through elements of the 30th Division. Task Force Jordan would take Stoumont, while the primary objective of clearing the road from La Gleize to Stoumont was handed to Task Force Lovelady.

The meticulously coordinated actions of these three task forces working in conjunction with the 30th Division would eventually hem in and eliminate *Kampfgruppe Peiper*'s foray in the west. The situation would culminate on Christmas Eve, 1944, in the village of La Gleize. Peiper's situation had become untenable. Surrounded and outnumbered on all sides by American forces, he was compelled to abandon his last vehicles and walk through the woods back to his own lines. At 03:00 hours on 24 December, an enemy foot column led by SS Lieutenant Colonel Peiper moved out of La Gleize. A group of 171 American prisoners were left behind to fend for themselves. The escaping Germans numbered around 800 and they left at intervals in small groups. They crossed the Amblève River on a small highway bridge south of La Gleize. Peiper left behind a team of demolition experts to destroy what remaining vehicles he had. At 05:00 hours, the first German tank was destroyed, and within 30 minutes the area formerly occupied by the *kampfgruppe* became a derelict sea of fiercely burning vehicles. As things transpired, they were in such a hurry to get away from La Gleize that a number of these vehicles remained intact. Peiper would spend the rest of the war recovering from battle fatigue.

On that same day, 24 December, Sankt Vith fell to attacking German forces, but it was already too late for them to take serious advantage of the situation. From his HQ in Vielsalm, 18th Airborne Corps commander General Matthew Ridgeway ordered the withdrawal of US forces within the 'Fortified Goose Egg' to positions behind General Gavin's 82nd Airborne. Most of the troops there were completely unaware of Montgomery's appointment when he sent them a personal message that read: 'You have accomplished your mission, a mission well done. It is time to withdraw, with all honour.' Once Monty had, in his words, 'tidied up the battlefield,' he could now prepare his offensive.

William H. Tucker, I Company, 3rd Battalion, 505th PIR, 82nd Airborne, said, 'During late morning of December 24, 1944, Capt. Archie McPheeters Jr. received the order to pull back from the Salm River, all the way to Basse-Bodeux. Word came down that Montgomery had ordered a major pullback of the 82nd Airborne Division to "tidy up the lines". We were furious! We held a secure, almost impregnable position along the Salm River, and had beaten off major elements of a German SS

Panzer Division. All our three platoons held the high ground, the idea of giving up captured ground to "tidy up the battlefield" was never accepted by the ranks of the 82nd Airborne, it was outrageous! But orders are orders, and they are meant to be carried out. It was planned to move the main body of I Company, assisted by two trucks (for ammo and supplies) at about 20:00 on Christmas Eve. Part of 2nd Platoon (about ten men) was to provide a rearguard at both the river line and the railroad until first light, the three 60 mm mortar squads were ordered to be united into one sole operating group (as in Holland, and despite narrow roads and thick woods). I was to supervise all three mortar gunners, hoping that the radios would work in case a fight developed and that they would remain fully operational in this hilly and wooded terrain.'

The most decorated airborne trooper of World War II, Lt. James 'Maggie' Megellas, often said that one of the reasons his 'H' company was so successful was due to someone whom he considered to be the best scout anyone could have.

Albert Tarbell, Company H, 504th Parachute Infantry Regiment, 82nd Airborne Division, was a full blood Mohawk Indian who had joined the army from the Mohawk Indian Reservation at Hogansbur, New York State. He was the first Mohawk in the 82nd Airborne Division during World War II, and he felt perfectly at home among the hills and pine forests around the Amblève valley. During an interview he said, 'Christmas Day we were set up on a defensive line. Our lines of communication were very long. We had lines to the battalion from our company, to the platoons, and to the O.P. [observation post]. We started getting hit by German patrols later on in the afternoon and throughout the day and evening. It was always difficult to maintain line communications whenever we received artillery fire. But we could revert to the radio as far as battalion. We were able to maintain good communications to the platoons, either by line or runner. H Company sent out patrols after the action and returned with prisoners. There were three of them, whom another trooper and myself took to battalion. As we arrived at the command post, Colonel Cook was outside and saw us come in with the prisoners. He ordered us over to him, and I thought he was going to kill them. They thought so too. He took out his .45 cal. and stuck it into the first SS guy's mouth, and they went down on their knees fast. They certainly did not look like supermen then! What a Christmas Day that was. No turkey, hardly any water for coffee. Later, we did get some water for coffee by melting snow.'

Bill Hannigan served with the same unit. He said that the SS prisoners were executed: 'Where could we put them? We were surrounded. So we took them into the woods and popped them one in the skull.'

'We met the Germans three miles from the Meuse River, and all hell broke loose,' said Myles Covey of the US 2nd Armored Division. 'The Germans had the 9th Panzer Division and the 2nd Panzer Division spearheading. On December 24 the most decisive battle took place. As a medic, you did what you had to do. I did not have to treat many wounded, since I was back with the artillery. We had three battalions of artillery in our division, and they would call us on the radio, and the artillery would fire shots at them. Most of the time, we were within eyesight of the German tanks. The tanks and the infantry had more casualties than the artillery did, since they were at the head of the spearhead. With a number of guns knocked out and captured, the British could account for 100 per cent of the 2nd Panzer Division being wiped out.'

While US forces on the northern shoulder began slowly but surely eradicating all German penetrations and mopping up stragglers, remaining German units in the field received a spurious order from their high command: 'All units to Bastogne.' The strategy for reaching Antwerp had failed and all that was left was a 'limited objective strategy' designed to inflict as much damage as possible before the inevitable retreat. Bastogne assumed a significance disproportionate to its actual military importance because of the powerful Allied propaganda generated by the siege and ensuing battles to take it. The city came to embody and encapsulate a strategic microclimate inside the perimeter of the Battle of the Bulge.

The British army's contribution in the Battle of the Bulge was considerably less than the American. It was quintessentially and inarguably an American battle, won by Americans. However, Monty wasted no time in ordering the British 30 Corps to pivot from the Netherlands and head towards the combat zone, to occupy defensive positions between Givet and Maastricht, in order to prevent the Germans from crossing the Meuse River. By 22 December, the 51st Highland Division, along with the 53rd Welsh Division, and the 29th and 33rd Armoured Brigades had reached their objectives and established their positions. The British 6th Airborne Division which, owing to inclement weather, was brought to the Ardennes

William 'Bill' Hannigan was with H Co, 1st Battalion, 504th Parachute Infantry, 82nd Airborne Division. He was one of the US paratroopers who took the fight to the SS.

in canal barges and trucks, followed later. The 6th Airborne Division was placed between Dinant and Namur under the command of the British 30 Corps and ordered to attack the apex of the German salient.

'We had our Christmas dinner in the "Chateau Ardennes", and it was a very pleasant way of enjoying Christmas, especially as there was a lot of snow around us, one got the festive feeling,' a British paratrooper recalled. 'Our battalion received an order to move to attack a village called Bure, and then secure another village. I was sent for by my C.O, and briefed. I was commander of "A" Company. The plan was to spend one night in Pondrome and then go by transport to Resteigne. There we would de bus and march to Tellin. There were six inches of snow and it was cold, below freezing, with ice on the roads, but the men were in good heart. We marched to a wood, which overlooked Bure, our first objective. We formed upon the start line and looked down on this silent and peaceful village. The Germans knew we were there; they were waiting for us, and as soon as we started to break cover I looked up and I could see about a foot above my head the branches of trees being shattered by intense machine-gun fire and mortaring.

'By about 21:00 on the evening of 5 January we had the whole village in our hands, with my company eliminating the last enemy post. We took up defensive positions, but that same night we were told to withdraw. We found out afterwards that the 7th Battalion had come in from a different direction, met with little resistance and taken Grupont. It meant that we did not have to go any farther. So very early on the morning of the 6th, just after midnight, I got all my company together and we withdrew to Tellin, very wet, very tired and unshaven. The battalion lost about 68 men killed, and about half of them were from my company. They were buried in a field in Bure by our Padre, Whitfield Foy, a few days later.'*

That Christmas Eve in 1944, during the wee small hours, a couple of miles from the Meuse River town of Dinant, the 3rd Royal Tank Regiment, supported by US tanks and the RAF, crossed the Meuse River to confront a column of German 2nd Panzer. This was the first practical encounter between British and German troops during the Battle of the Bulge and it signalled the high-water mark of the German army in their vain attempt

---

* Source: Checkerboard Newsletter, March 1993

to navigate the river and reach Antwerp. Shortly thereafter, the port of Antwerp was abandoned as the primary tactical objective of the German forces and replaced with Bastogne.

From the end of December and the beginning of January 1945, the bulge was being reduced from three angles, from north, south and west. This is when the real Ardennes winter finally arrived. Temperatures frequently dropped below -20°C (-4°F) and blizzard conditions caused white-outs throughout the combat zone. Assisted by Sherman Firefly tanks from the Fife and Forfar Yeomanry, the 5th Parachute Brigade attacked the village of Bure at the western perimeter of the bulge. The attack that commenced on 3 January 1945 resulted in severe casualties as bitter fighting raged for three whole days in atrocious winter conditions. German infantry and tank attacks were repeatedly repelled until reinforcements from C Company 2nd Ox and Bucks, and additional tanks from the 23rd Hussars, helped to capture the village and press east. There's a plaque in the Ardennes town of La Roche that commemorates the meeting between the US 84th Infantry Division 'Railsplitters' and the British Black Watch Regiment, 51st Highland Division, and marks the exact location where that meeting occurred on 11 January 1945.

'When we first set off, I vividly remember seeing Hasso von Manteuffel standing on a Panther tank shouting, "*Schneller, schneller!*" [faster, faster] as we passed toward the Belgian border. It was bitterly cold, and there was no heating in our half-track, so we did as best we could to keep warm,' said Hans Herbst of the 116th German Panzer 'Greyhound' (*Windhund*) Division, one of the most respected divisions in the German army. 'Shortly after crossing the border, we picked up supplies abandoned by the Amis. We had plenty to eat, and I had many cartons of Lucky Strikes in the half-track. We were about a mile from Wibrin heading direct west when the Panther G in front spotted a Sherman beside the church in Wibrin. He fired a round that glanced off the front of the Sherman. Through my field glasses, I saw the whole action.

'My platoon disembarked from the half-track and moved in the direction of the Sherman. As we closed in, the Panther fired another round and another that both missed the target. The Sherman then turned to return fire; the turret slowly turned, and it pointed directly at us, and then there was a huge explosion. The Sherman was out of action. We didn't know what had caused it, though. It was only when I got closer to inspect the damage that I saw what had happened. The first shot had glanced off the front and slightly bent the cannon on the turret of the Sherman so that when he attempted to return fire, his shell got stuck and exploded the turret. It was a very lucky escape. We continued west after that. Our division was one of the few that almost made it to the river Meuse. We also fought the British near Hotton. It was a savage firefight there, and many of our comrades were killed. That was the worst fighting we encountered during the whole offensive.'

While the British were mopping up in the west, a combined effort from the US 1st and 3rd Armies was hitting the northern and southern penetrations along the German promontory into the Ardennes. This massive pincer movement eventually began to cauterize and envelop the whole line. It's important to note that although American forces provided the bulk of men and materials in the Battle of the Bulge, Belgian and French Special Forces also fought hard and provided excellent reconnaissance throughout.

At the end of 1944 Hitler sensed that his attempt to divide the Allies piecemeal had failed, but in an attempt to deflect attention from the Ardennes, he ordered a reduced offensive, Operation Northwind (*Nordwind*) in north-eastern France, which began on New Year's Day and petered out on 25 January 1945. The primary purpose was to lure Allied troops away from the Ardennes sector. Hitler erroneously assumed that once this operation had succeeded, he would be able to resume his drive to the Meuse River. It became the last German offensive in the west.

At the time it occurred British intelligence were way ahead of the game and expertly deciphering the whole German plan. They relayed all Hitler's military directives directly to General Eisenhower. There was a brief hiatus in the Battle of the Bulge at the beginning of January as foggy weather dominated once more and all roads became intractable due to ice. Despite the inclement weather conditions, the Allies maintained the pressure and gave Hitler no alternative than to recall his tanks and troops back to Germany. This signalled the stuttering end of the Battle of the Bulge.

At this juncture Monty organized a press conference at his 21st Army Group headquarters in the Flemish Belgian town of Zonhoven. In front of the assembled press corps he used large maps to indicate how he had personally won the Battle of the Bulge, even though the actual battle hadn't even concluded. He ranted for over an hour about how he personally 'employed the whole available power of the British group of armies: this power was brought into play very gradually and in such a way that it would not interfere with the American lines of communications. Finally, it was put into battle with a bang and today British divisions are fighting hard on the right flank of the United States 1st Army. You thus have the picture of British troops fighting on both sides of American forces who have suffered a hard blow. The battle has been most interesting; I think possibly one of the most interesting and tricky battles I have ever handled.'

This was understandably not well received by American commanders at SHAEF and those who were still fighting in the active combat zones. General Bradley was livid when he heard about Monty's impromptu press conference. Even though he was almost exploding with indignation, he found the time to help set the record straight and organize his own press conference. Even Churchill was compelled to intervene when he practised his version of damage limitation by giving a speech to the House of Commons on 18 January 1945, whereupon he graciously paid tribute to the American soldiers and warned, 'Care must be taken in telling our proud tale not to claim for the British Army an undue share of what is undoubtedly the greatest American battle of the war.' His words were in fact a veiled reprimand against Monty.

Elements of the US 1st and 3rd Armies met on 16 January 1945, in the small, devastated town of Houffalize. The pincer had closed. The Battle of the Bulge was Germany's last major western offensive. The German army suffered greatly as a result of the fighting in the Ardennes, and even though they would continue to fight for five more months, this defeat in the winter of 1944–45 sapped all remaining offensive capability and handed the tactical and strategic initiative to the Allies. The potential threat of a further German *Blitzkrieg* had been effectively eradicated. However, the German offensive in the Ardennes had never seriously presented a long-term threat to the Allies. Hitler's restricted ability to exploit any potential strategic advantage that the Battle of the Bulge could have given would eventually have been seriously diminished due to the rampant advances of Red Army hordes in the east. Diverting troops and equipment from the east to stage a futile offensive in the west simply allowed the Soviets to increase their already relentless pressure.

Although the initial contribution of the Allied air forces failed to impact significantly on the defence of the Ardennes, they eventually succeeded in almost entirely eradicating what remained of the German Luftwaffe. Hitler was delusional and grossly misinformed by his Nazi sycophants. He placed his distorted faith in 'super-weapons' such as the V-1 and V-2 rockets, and the Me 262 jet bombers, believing that these would turn the tide of the war in his favour; in reality, their manufacture only sapped the damaged German economy. They were desperate products to appease an increasingly desperate man. The rockets inflicted damage, there's no doubt about that, but by the end of 1944 the damage inflicted on German cities by Allied bomber command killed on average 13,536 German citizens every month, culminating by the end of the war in the deaths of over 400,000. It was recently discovered that the atmospheric undulations caused by explosions resulting from Allied bombing raids actually impacted the ionosphere, and each raid released the energy of approximately 300 lightning strikes.

Although Allied bombing alone wasn't enough to subdue the Third Reich, by the spring of 1945 it was beginning to fracture both externally and internally. After the Allied victory at the Battle of the Bulge it would only be a matter of time before the Nazi regime imploded.

Opposing Armies

American units

16 December 1944

12TH ARMY GROUP

Lieutenant General Omar N. Bradley

(Chief of Staff: Maj. Gen. Leven C. Allen, HQ: Luxembourg)

US 1ST ARMY

Lt. Gen. Courtney H. Hodges

(Chief of Staff, Maj. Gen. William B. Kean, HQ 16 December: Spa)

Troop B, 125 Cavalry Recon. Sqn.

5 Belgian Fusilier Bn., 99 Inf. Bn. (Norwegian-Americans)

526 Armored Inf. Bn., 143 and 413 Anti Aircraft Artillery Bns.

825 Tank Destroyer Bn. (towed), 9 Canadian Forestry Co.

61, 158, 299, 300 and 1278 Engineer Combat Bns.

V Corps.

Maj. Gen. Leonard T. Gerow, HQ: Eupen

51, 112, 146, 202, 254, 291, 296 Engineer Combat Bns.

186 and 941 Field Artillery Bns., 62 Armored FA Bn.

102 Cavalry Group, Mechanized (38 and 102 Cavalry Recon. Sqns.)

78th Infantry Division (Maj. Gen. Edwin P. Parker)

309, 310 and 311 Inf. Regts.

95 Armored FA Bn., 709 Tank Bn., 893 Tank Destroyer Bn.

99th Infantry Division (Maj. Gen. Walter E. Lauer)

393, 394 and 395 Inf. Regts.

196, 776 and 924 FA Bns., 801 TD Bn. (towed)

2nd Infantry Division (Maj. Gen. Walter M. Robertson)

9, 23 and 38 Inf. Regts.

16 Armored FA Bn., 18, 200, 955 and 987 FA Bns.

741 Tank Bn., 644 (M10) and 612 (towed) TD Bns.

CCB, 9th Armored Division (Brig. Gen. William H. Hoge)

27 Armored Inf. Bn., 14 Tank Bn., 16 Armored FA Bn.

VIII Corps

Maj. Gen. Troy H. Middleton, HQ: Bastogne

35, 44, 159 and 168 Engineer Combat Bns.

333, 559, 561, 578, 740, 770, 771, 965 and 969 FA Bns.

274 Armored FA Bn.

14 Cavalry Group, Mechanized (18 and 32 Cavalry Recon. Sqns.)
(Col. Mark A. Devine)

106th Infantry Division (Maj. Gen. Alan W. Jones)

422, 423 and 424 Inf. Regts.

28th Infantry Division (Maj. Gen. Norman D. Cota)

109, 110 and 112 Inf. Regts.

630 TD Bn. (towed), 687 FA Bn., 707 Tank Bn.

4th Infantry Division (Maj. Gen. Raymond O. Barton)

8, 12 and 22 Inf. Regt., 81 and 174 FA Bns.

802 (towed) and 803 (M10) TD Bns., 70 Tank Bn.

CCA and CCR, 9th Armored Division (Maj. Gen. John W. Leonard)

52 & 60 Armored Inf. Bns., 2 & 19 Tank Bns, 3 & 73 Armored FA Bns.

German units
16 December 1944

OB WEST

Generalfeldmarschall Gerd von Rundstedt

(Chief of Staff: *General der Kavallerie Siegfried Westphal*)

ARMY GROUP 'B'

Generalfeldmarschall Walther Model

(Chief of Staff: *General der Infanterie Hans Krebs*)

GERMAN 6TH PANZER ARMY (NORTHERN SHOULDER)

Oberstgruppenführer Sepp Dietrich

(Chief of Staff: *SS Brigadeführer Fritz Krämer*)

Fallschirmjäger Bn. (Oberst Freiherr Friedrich-August von der Heydte)

506 Heavy Panzer Bn. (Tiger II)

2 Flak Division, 4 *Todt* Brigade

I SS-Panzer Corps

Gruppenführer Hermann Priess

388 and 402 *VolksArtillerie Korps*, 4 and 9 *VolksWerfer* Brigades

1 SS-*Leibstandarte* Panzer Division (Oberführer Wilhelm Mohnke)

1 SS-Panzer Regt., 1 and 2 SS-*Panzergrenadier* Regts

12th SS-*Hitlerjugend* Panzer Division (Standartenführer Hugo Kraas)

12 SS-Panzer Regt., 25 and 26 SS-*Panzergrenadier* Regts.

3 *Fallschirmjager* Division (Generalmajor Walther Wadehn)

5, 6 and 9 *Fallschirmjäger* Regts.

12 *Volksgrenadier* Division (Generalmajor Gerhard Engel)

27 Fusilier, 48 and 49 *Volksgrenadier* Regts.

277 *Volksgrenadier* Division (Oberst Wilhelm Viebig)

289, 990 and 991 *Volksgrenadier* Regiments

150 Panzer Brigade (Obersturmbannführer Otto Skorzeny)

LXVII Corps

Generalleutnant Otto Hitzfeld

405 *VolksArtillerie Korps*, 17 *VolksWerfer* Brigade

3rd *Panzergrenadier* Division (Generalmajor Walther Denkert)

103 Panzer Bn., 8 and 29 *Panzergrenadier* Regts

246 *Volksgrenadier* Division (Oberst Peter Körte)

352, 404 and 689 *Volksgrenadier* Regts.

272 *Volksgrenadier* Division (Oberst Georg Kosmalla)

980, 981 and 982 *Volksgrenadier* Regiments

326 *Volksgrenadier* Division (Oberst Erwin Kaschner)

751, 752 and 753 *Volksgrenadier* Regts.

II SS-Panzer Corps

Obergruppenführer Willi Bittrich

410 *VolksArtillerie Korps*, 502 SS-Heavy Artillery Bn.

2nd SS-*Das Reich* Panzer Division (Brigadeführer Heinz Lammerding)

2 SS-Panzer Regt., 3 and 4 SS-*Panzergrenadier* Regts.

9th SS-Hohenstaufen Panzer Division (Oberführer Sylvester Stadler)

9 SS-Panzer Regt., 19 and 20 SS-*Panzergrenadier* Regts.

GERMAN 5TH PANZER ARMY (CENTRE)

General der Panzertruppen Freiherr Hasso von Manteuffel

(Chief of Staff: Generalmajor Carl Wagener)

LXVI Corps

General der Artillerie Walther Lucht

460 Heavy Artillery Bn., 16 *VolksWerfer* Brigade

18 *Volksgrenadier* Division (Oberst Günther Hoffmann-Schönborn)

293, 294 and 295 *Volksgrenadier* Regts.

62 *Volksgrenadier* Division (Oberst Friedrich Kittel)

164, 193 and 190 *Volksgrenadier* Regts.

XLVII Panzer Corps

General der Panzertruppen Freiherr Heinrich von Lüttwitz

766 *VolksArtillerie Korps*, 15 *VolksWerfer* Brigade, 182 Flak Regt.

2 Panzer Division (Oberst Meinrad von Lauchert)

3 Panzer Regt., 2 and 304 *Panzergrenadier* Regts.

9 Panzer Division (Generalmajor Harald von Elverfeldt)

33 Panzer Regt., 10 and 11 *Panzergrenadier* Regts

Panzer Lehr (Generalleutnant Fritz Bayerlein)

130 Panzer Regt., 901 and 902 *Panzergrenadier* Regts.

26 *Volksgrenadier* Division (Oberst Heinz Kokott)

39 Fusilier, 77 and 78 *Volksgrenadier* Regts.

Fuhrer-Begleit-Brigade (Oberst Otto Remer)

LVIII Panzer Corps

General der Panzertruppen Walther Krüger

401 *VolksArtillerie Korps*, 7 *VolksWerfer* Brigade, 1 Flak Regt.

116 (*Windhund*) Panzer Division (Generalmajor Siegfried von Waldenburg)

16 Panzer Regt., 60 and 156 *Panzergrenadier* Regts.

560 *Volksgrenadier* Division (Oberst Rudolf Langhauser)

1128, 1129 and 1130 *Volksgrenadier* Regts.

XXXIX Panzer Corps (committed end of December)

Generalleutnant Karl Decker

167 *Volksgrenadier* Division (Generalleutnant Hans-Kurt Höcker)

331, 339 and 387 *Volksgrenadier* Regts.

GERMAN 7TH ARMY (SOUTHERN SHOULDER)

General der Panzertruppen Erich Brandenberger

(Chief of Staff: Generalmajor Freiherr Rudolf von Gersdorff)

LXXX Corps

General der Infanterie Franz Beyer

408 *VolksArtillerie Korps*, 8 *VolksWerfer* Brigade, 2 and *Lehr Werfer* Regts.

212 *Volksgrenadier* Division (Generalmajor Franz Sensfuss)

316, 320 and 423 *Volksgrenadier* Regts.

276 *Volksgrenadier* Division (Genlt Kurt Möhring/Oberst Hugo Dempwolff)

986, 987 and 988 *Volksgrenadier* Regts.

340 *Volksgrenadier* Division (Oberst Theodor Tolsdorff)

208, 212 and 226 *Volksgrenadier* Regts.

LXXXV Corps

General der Infanterie Baptist Kniess

406 *VolksArtillerie Korps*, 18 *VolksWerfer* Brigade

11 *Sturmgewehr* (StuG) Brigade (Oberstleutnant Georg Hollunder)

5 *Fallschirmjäger* Division (Oberst Ludwig Heilmann)

13, 14 and 15 *Fallschirmjäger* Regts.

352 *Volksgrenadier* Division (Oberst Erich Schmidt)

914, 915 and 916 *Volksgrenadier* Regts.

79 *Volksgrenadier* Division (Oberst Alois Weber)

208, 212 and 226 *Volksgrenadier* Regts.

LIII Corps (committed 22 December)

General der Kavallerie Edwin von Rothkirch und Trach

9 *Volksgrenadier* Division (Oberst Werner Kolb)

36, 57 and 116 *Volksgrenadier* Regts.

15 *Panzergrenadier* Division (Oberst Hans-Joachim Deckert)

115 Panzer Bn, 104 and 115 *Panzergrenadier* Regts.

Führer-Grenadier-Brigade (Oberst Hans Joachim Kahler)

Allied Forces. Battle of the Bulge

1 January 1945

12TH ARMY GROUP

Lt. Gen. Omar N. Bradley

(Chief of Staff: Maj. Gen. Leven C. Allen, HQ: Luxembourg)

US 1ST ARMY

Lt. Gen. Courtney H. Hodges

Chief of Staff: Maj. Gen. William B. Kean,

HQ: Chaudfontaine /Troyes)

V Corps

Maj. Gen. Leonard T. Gerow, HQ: Eupen

102 Cavalry Group, Mechanized (38 and 102 Cavalry Recon Sqns)

1st Infantry Division (Brig. Gen. Clift Andrus)

16, 18 and 26 Inf. Regts., 745 Tank Bn., 634 and 703 TD Bns.

2nd Infantry Division (Maj. Gen. Walter M. Robertson)

9, 23 and 38 Inf. Regts., 741 Tank Bn., 612 and 644 TD Bns.

9th Infantry Division (Maj. Gen. Louis A. Craig)

39, 47 and 60 Inf. Regts., 38 Cavalry Recon. Sqn. (attached), 746 Tank Bn.

78th Infantry Division (Maj. Gen. Edwin P. Parker)

309, 310 and 311 Inf. Regts., 709 Tank Bn., 628 and 893 TD Bns.

CCR, 5th Armored Division (attached), 2nd Ranger Bn. (attached)

99th Infantry Division (Maj. Gen. Walter E. Lauer)

393, 394 and 395 Inf. Regts., 801 TD Bn.

VII Corps

Maj. Gen. J. Lawton Collins

4th Cavalry Group, Mechanized (4th and 24th Cavalry Recon Sqns.)

29 Inf. Regt., 509 Parachute (Para) Inf. Bn.

740 Tank Bn., 759 Light Tank Bn., 635 TD Bn.

2 Armored Division (Maj. Gen. Ernest N. Harmon)

41 Armored Inf. Regt., 66 and 67 Armored Regts.

3 Armored Division (Maj. Gen. Maurice Rose)

36 Armored Inf. Regt., 32 and 33 Armored Regts.

83 Infantry Division (Maj. Gen. Robert C. Macon)

329, 330, and 331 Inf. Regts., 774 Tank Bn.

84 Infantry Division (Brig. Gen. Alexander R. Bolling)

333, 334, and 335 Inf. Regs., 771 Tank Bn.

XVIII Airborne Corps

Maj. Gen. Matthew B. Ridgway

14 Cavalry Group, Mechanized (18 and 32 Cavalry Recon. Sqns.)

7 Armored Division (Brig. Gen. Robert W. Hasbrouck)

23, 38 and 48 Armored Inf. Bns., 17, 31, and 40 Tank Bns.

434, 440 and 489 Armored FA Bns.

30 Infantry Division (Maj. Gen. Leland S. Hobbs)

117, 119 and 120 Inf. Regts., 743 Tank Bn., 99th Inf. Bn. (attached)

517 Para. Inf. Regt. (attached), 526 Armored Inf. Bn. (attached)

75 Infantry Division (Maj. Gen. Fay B. Prickett)

289, 290 and 29 Inf. Regts., 750 Tank Bn.

82 Airborne Division (Maj. Gen. James M. Gavin)

504, 505, and 508 Para. Inf. Regts., 325 Glider Inf. Regt.

551 Para. Inf. Bn. (attached)

US 3RD ARMY

Lt. Gen. George S. Patton, Jr

Chief of Staff: Brig. Gen. Hobart R. Gay, HQ: Nancy

III Corps

Maj. Gen. John B. Millikin, HQ: Arlon

6 Cavalry Group, Mechanized (6 and 26 Cavalry Recon. Sqns.)

4 Armored Division (Maj. Gen. Hugh J. Gaffey)

10, 51 and 53 Armored Inf. Bns., 8, 35 and 37 Tank Bns.

6 Armored Division (Maj. Gen. Robert W. Grow)

9, 44 and 50 Armored Inf. Bns., 15, 68 and 69 Tank Bns.

26 Infantry Division (Maj. Gen. Willard S. Paul)

101, 104 and 328 Inf. Regts., 735 Tank Bn.

35 Infantry Division (Maj. Gen. Paul W. Baade)

134, 137 and 320 Inf. Regts.

90 Infantry Division (Maj. Gen. James A. Van Fleet)

357, 358 and 359 Inf. Regts.

VIII Corps

Maj. Gen. Troy H. Middleton, HQ: Neufchâteau

9 Armored Division (Maj. Gen. John W. Leonard)

27, 52 and 60 Armored Inf. Bns., 2, 14 and 19 Tank Bns.

11 Armored Division (Brig. Gen. Charles S. Kilburn)

21, 55 and 63 Armored Inf. Bns., 22, 41 and 42 Tank Bns.

17 Airborne Division (Maj. Gen. William M. Miley)

507 and 513 Para. Inf. Regts., 193 and 194 Glider Inf. Regts.

28 Infantry (Maj. Gen. Norman D. Cota)

109, 110 and 112 Inf. Regts., 707 Tank Bn.

87 Infantry Division (Brig. Gen. John M. Lentz)

345, 346 and 347 Inf. Regts., 761st (Black Panthers) Tank Bn.

101 Airborne Division

(Brig. Gen. Anthony C. McAuliffe/Maj. Gen. Maxwell D. Taylor)

501, 502 and 506 Para. Inf. Regts., 327th Glider Inf. Regt.

1 Battalion, 401 Glider Inf. Regt.

XII Corps

Maj. Gen. Manton S. Eddy

2 Cavalry Group, Mechanized (2 and 42 Cavalry Recon. Sqns.)

4 Infantry Division (Maj. Gen. Raymond O. Barton)

8, 12 and 22 Inf. Regts., 70 Tank Bn.

5 Infantry Division (Maj. Gen. S. Leroy Irwin)

2, 10 and 11 Inf. Regts., 737 Tank Bn.

10 Armored Division (Maj. Gen. William H. H. Morris, Jr)

20, 54 and 61 Armored Inf. Bns., 3, 11, and 21 Tank Bns.

80 Infantry Division (Maj. Gen. Horace L. McBride)

317, 318 and 319 Inf. Regts., 702 Tank Bn.

21ST ARMY GROUP

Field Marshal Sir Bernard L. Montgomery

(Chief of Staff: Maj. Gen. F.W. de Guingand, HQ: Zonhoven)

BRITISH 2ND ARMY

General Sir Miles Dempsey

(Chief of Staff: Brigadier Harold 'Pete' Pyman)

XXX Corps

Lt. Gen. Sir Brian Horrocks

6 Airborne Division (Maj. Gen. Eric L. Bols)

3 and 5 Para. Brigades, 6 Air Landing Brigade

51 Highland Division (Maj. Gen. Tom G. Rennie)

152, 153 and 154 Inf. Brigades

53 Welsh Division (Maj. Gen. Robert K. Ross)

71, 158 and 160 Inf. Brigades

29 Armoured Brigade (Brig. Roscoe B. Harvey)

(3 Royal Tank Regiment, 2 Fife & Forfar Yeomanry, 23 Hussars, 8 Rifle Brigade)

33rd Armoured Brigade (Brig. H.B. Scott)

(144 Royal Armoured Corps, 1 Northamptonshire Yeomanry, 1 East Riding Yeomanry)

Bibliography

AUTHOR INTERVIEWS
Robert Kennedy
Dorothy Barre
Allan P. Atwell
Albert Tarbell
W. D. Crittenberger
Ted Paluch
William Hannigan
Ralph K. Manley
Francis S. Currey
Frank Towers
Frank Denius
Darel Parker
George Schneider
Hans Herbst
Manfred Toon Thorn
Gunter Adams
Hans Baumann
John R. Schaffner
Arthur Letchford
Albert Honowitz

AUTHOR'S CORRESPONDENCE
Personal memoirs and audiotapes
John Kline (http://ice.mm.com/user/jpk/battle.htm)
Frank Towers
James L. Cooley (Robert Cooley's transcription)
Phil Burge
Rudolf von Ribbentrop

INTERNET SOURCES

http://users.skynet.be/wielewaal/Chaumont.htm

www.3ad.com (3rd Armored Division History Foundation)

www.11tharmoreddivision.com (11th Armored Division Association)

www.bloodybucket.be (*Groupe Belge de Reconstitution*

Historique Militaire)

www.indianamilitary.org (Indiana History Organization)

BOOKS AND ARTICLES

Adam, Günter. 9th SS-Panzer Division *Hohenstaufe, Ich habe meine Pflicht erfüllt!: Ein Junker der Waffen-SS berichtet* ('I did my duty: Reports from a young man in the Waffen-SS'). Riesa, Germany: Nation & Wissen, 2012.

Arn, Edward C. *Arn's War: Memoirs of a World War II Infantryman, 1940–1946*. Akron: University of Akron Press, 2005.

Atkinson, Rick. *Danger Zone. World War II* (July–August 2013)

Collins, Michael, and Martin King. *Voices of the Bulge: Untold Stories from Veterans of the Battle of the Bulge*. Zenith, 2011.

Collins, Michael and Martin King. *Warriors of the 106th*. Casemate, 2018.

Collins, Michael, Col. Jason Nulton and Martin King. *To War with the 4th – A century of frontline combat*. Casemate, 2015.

Collins, Michael, David Hilmore and Martin King. *The Fighting 30th – They called them Roosevelt's SS*. Casemate, 2016.

Martin King. *Searching for Augusta*. Lyonpress, 2018.

Collins, Michael, and Martin King. *Tigers of Bastogne*. Casemate, 2014.

Peter Caddick Adams. *Snow and Steel*. Oxford University Press, 2015.

Robert Merriam. *Dark December*. Ziff Davis publishing company, 1947.

Cooke, David, and Wayne Evans. *Kampfgruppe Peiper at the Battle of the Bulge.* Mechanicsburg, Pa. Stackpole, 2008.

Featherston, Alwyn. *Battle for Mortain: The 30th Infantry Division Saves the Breakout, August 7–12, 1944.* New York: Presidio, 1998.

Folkestad, William B. *The View from the Turret: the 743rd Tank Battalion during World War II.* Shippensburg, Pa. Burd Street, 1996.

Ford, Ken, and Howard Gerrard. *The Rhine Crossings, 1945.* New York: Osprey, 2007.

Harrison, Gordon A. *Cross-Channel Attack.* Washington: CMP, 1951.

Hewitt, Robert L. *Work Horse of the Western Front: The Story of the 30th Infantry Division.* Washington, D.C.: Infantry Journal, 1946.

Higgins, David R. *The Roer River Battles: Germany's Stand at the Westwall, 1944–45.* Havertown, Pa: Casemate, 2010.

Hymel, Kevin. 'Strong Stand Atop Mortain', *WWII History* (July 2012): 48–55.

Lewis, James M. 'Repulse of the German Counterattack Aimed at Avranches, 7–11 August 1944,' dated 25 August 1944

Charles B. MacDonald, *The Siegfried Line Campaign* (Washington, D.C.: Center of Military History, 1993), 307, reproduced at http://www.history.army.mil/html/books/007/7-7-1/CMH_Pub_7-7-1.pdf.

McArthur, Charles W. 'Operations Analysis in the U.S. Army Eighth Air Force' in Pallud, Jean-Paul, *The Battle of the Bulge Then and Now.* London: Battle of Britain Prints International, 1984.

Reardon, Mark J. *Victory at Mortain: Stopping Hitler's Panzer Counteroffensive.* Lawrence: University Press of Kansas, 2002.

Ribbentrop, Rudolf von. *Joachim von Ribbentrop: Mein Vater: Erlebnisse und Erinnerungen.* Graz, Austria: Arles, 2008.

Sanford, Marion, and Jeff Rogers, *Old Hickory Recon: Memories of the 30th Infantry Division, 1943–1945.* Wetumpka, Ala.: Schweinhund, 2012.

Vannoy, Allyn R., and Jay Karamales. *Against the Panzers: United States Infantry versus German Tanks, 1944–1945*. Jefferson, N.C.: McFarland, 1996.

Weiss, Robert. *Fire Mission: The Siege at Mortain, Normandy, August 1944*. Shippensburg, Pa.: Burd Street, 2002.

Zaloga, Steven. *Battle of the Ardennes 1944 (1) St. Vith and the Northern Shoulder*. New York: Osprey, 2002.

Zaloga, Steven. *Operation Cobra 1944: Breakout from Normandy*. Westport, Conn.: Praeger, 2004.

Zaloga, Steven, and Steve Noon. *The Siegfried Line 1944–45: Battles on the German Frontier*. New York: Osprey, 2007.

http://www.thememoryproject.com/stories/WWII

Veteran stories Second World War Canada

http://www.hertsmemories.org.uk/content/herts-history/topics/wartime/wartime_potters_bar

http://memory.loc.gov/diglib/vhp/story/loc.natlib.afc2001001.16160/transcript?ID=mv0001

Index

Picture Credits

Getty Images: 53, 88, 93, 94, 100

Library of Congress: 78

Lovell Johns: 16, 176, 187, 196, 220

Martin King: 58, 62, 73, 84, 108, 115, 151, 161, 232

National Archives Records and Administration, United States: 20, 24, 29, 70, 74, 104, 184, 218

US Army Center of Military History: 146, 222, 226